The Oxford Movement

The Oxford Movement

A Thematic History of the Tractarians and Their Times

C. Brad Faught

The Pennsylvania State University Press
University Park, Pennsylvania

Library of Congress Cataloging-in-Publication Data

Faught, C. Brad.
The Oxford movement : a thematic history of the tractarians
and their times / C. Brad Faught.
p.   cm.
Includes bibliographical references and index.
ISBN 0-271-02249-3 (alk. paper)
1. Oxford movement.   I. Title.

BX5098 .F38 2003
283'.42'09034—dc21
2002153332

It is the policy of The Pennsylvania State
University Press to use acid-free paper.
Publications on uncoated stock satisfy the minimum
requirements of American National Standard
for Information Sciences—Permanence of Paper
for Printed Library Materials,
ANSI Z39.48–1992.

Contents

Preface and Acknowledgments

Well over a hundred and fifty years after its high point, the Oxford Movement remains a powerful example of religion in action. Led by four Oxford dons—John Henry Newman, John Keble, Richard Hurrell Froude, and Edward Bouverie Pusey—this Church of England catholic renewal movement was a seminal event in the religious, political, and Social history of mid-nineteenth-century Britain.

From evangelicalism to Tractarianism to the Social Christianity of the twentieth century, Oxford holds a vital place in the history of the Western Christian faith. And it was here, amidst the spires and quadrangles of Britain's first university near the outset of Queen Victoria's reign, that a group of dons—all sometime fellows of Oriel College—decided to lead a religious crusade against what they saw as the liberal and Erastian spirit of the age.

Beginning symbolically in 1833 with Keble's "National Apostasy" sermon and lasting formally until Newman's 1845 conversion to Roman Catholicism, the Oxford Movement—as this crusade came to be called—posed deep and far-reaching questions about the nature of the relationship between church and state, the catholic heritage of the Church of England, and the Church's social responsibility, especially in the new industrial society.[1] The Oxford men—or the Tractarians as they were called in reference to their publication *Tracts for the Times*—courted controversy from the outset. Their attack on the state for its insidious violation of sacred Church prerogatives exemplified by Parliament's passing of the Irish Church bill that year was a springboard for a sustained championing of the Church of England's independence. They traced this independence to the early church and to the Roman Catholic Church, its organic successor in Western Christendom. The Tractarians' slowly burgeoning belief in the necessity of reclaiming the catholic heritage of the Church of England put them on a collision course with Protestant churchmen and with evangelicals, both of whom in various ways viewed with suspicion or hostility the Tractarians' acceptance of catholic ecclesiastical, theological, and religious norms.

From 1833 to 1845, Newman, Keble, Froude, and Pusey shaped the religiopolitical debate and set in train the history of modern Anglo-Catholicism. Much of the sharpest controversy and the most compelling drama occurred during these years. From their Oxford base, this Group of Four divided the Church of England, a division that can be felt even today. But it was during the 1830s and 1840s that their impact was strongest and most important; and therefore, any study of the Oxford Movement must return to this period.Of course, as in any movement, leaders, fellow travelers, followers, and observers enter, stay, and leave the scene of the action. This is especially true of the Oxford foursome, who displayed, over the dozen years concentrated on here, a not-altogether-comfortable unity. Nevertheless, these men found at different times and over different issues a startling commonality of purpose that reduced or even eliminated internal dissension.

The idea for giving this book a thematic structure came from reading Linda Colley's *Britons: Forging the Nation, 1707–1832* (1992). In setting out to explain how a "British" identity was constructed in the eighteenth and early nineteenth centuries, Colley examines certain themes which ran through the history of England, Scotland, Wales, and Ireland at that time. This thematic approach proved highly successful and, it seemed to me, provided an effective model for trying to draw together the many different strands of the history of the Oxford Movement. The result is this study, in which five themes are set out and elaborated in an attempt to synthesize a large amount of historical thinking—much of it recent—on the topic.

The literature on the Oxford Movement has lacked a modern, brief, synthetic, and accessible account of its main personalities, events, and issues.[2] The thematic approach adopted here is an attempt to encompass the Movement by examining it through the important categories of politics, religion and theology, friendship, society, and missions. Though I do stray on occasion from the 1833–45 chronology, I have tried to stay within the lifetimes of the original Tractarians themselves.

I wish to thank a number of people who have helped me throughout my work. First and foremost, I have been guided by the imaginative hand of Richard J. Helmstadter, who first suggested that I write on the Oxford Movement. He took a close interest in this book, for which I am grateful. I would like to thank also the Historical Society of the Episcopal Church (U.S.), whose grant allowed for a research trip to Oxford where I worked mostly in the peaceful and resource-rich library at Pusey House. My stay in Oxford was made comfortable by my old college, St. Antony's.

Peter J. Potter, editor-in-chief of Penn State University Press, has guided this project from the beginning. I would like to thank him and the other Press staff for their expert work. Paul Phillips, my friend and colleague at St. Francis Xavier University in Nova Scotia, suggested that I approach Peter with my manuscript. I am very glad I heeded his advice. Thanks, also, to the Press's two anonymous readers for their highly useful critique of the penultimate draft.

My wife, Rhonda Jansen, has been greatly supportive in a number of ways in the writing of this book, and our little daughter Claire pulled me back smartly always from the nineteenth century to the twenty-first.

1 *Politics*
CONTROVERSY AND PASSION

*I*n the beginning there was politics. As Owen Chadwick, the dean of historians of Victorian Christianity, wrote in his important essay, "The Mind of the Oxford Movement," first published in 1960: "It is safe to say that the Movement would not have taken the form which it took without the impetus of ecclesiastical and secular politics."[1] Traditionally, scholars of the Oxford Movement, as well as others, shied away from seeing the Movement in political terms, mostly because of its generally acknowledged religious character. In recent years, however, this reluctance has diminished, partly in response to the widening of historical inquiry generally, and partly in response to a lessening of intense party feeling within the Church of England. The result is that the Oxford Movement's pronounced political features have been the focus of a number of key contemporary studies. Most prominent among these are Terence Kenny's on the political thought of Newman, J.H.L. Rowlands's on the political and social thought of all the leading Tractarians, and Peter Nockles's on Anglican high churchmanship.[2] This chapter finds both its inspiration and its justification in these studies. Indeed, it may be argued that only through a proper understanding of the political life of Great Britain in the 1820s and 1830s can the origins and course of the Oxford Movement be fully understood. Politics, here defined essentially as relations between church and state, consumed the Oxford men in their early struggle. Consequently, any synthetic study of the Oxford Movement must begin with a treatment of the political environment of the time. In this respect, Dean Church's original conceptualization of the Oxford Movement's twelve-year span, while no longer definitive, remains especially useful.[3]

In 1815, Bonaparte's final defeat at Waterloo and exile to the distant South Atlantic island of St. Helena was met in Britain with almost unparalleled celebration. After twenty-three years of nearly continuous war and upheaval, at last Britain had entered a period of relative quiet, at least as far as relations with continental Europe were concerned. Such was not the case at home, however, in the cities and towns of a Britain presided over nominally by the sick and aging George III. Despite the initial celebrations surrounding Napoleon's defeat, the postwar years were marked by a good deal of social unrest brought on by economic depression and high inflation, epitomized by Manchester's 1819 Peterloo Massacre, where food riots turned violent, the soldiers were called out, and at the end of the clash eleven protesters lay dead. In the spirit of the day, politics became a theater of increasingly severe contest. Robert Banks Jenkinson, Lord Liverpool, the long-lived and long-suffering Tory prime minister, managed to stay in office for a remarkable fifteen years, from 1812 until 1827. But political stability at the top masked considerable social instability below. By the late 1820s this mask had been torn off, and with the fall of the Liverpool government began five years of intense political and parliamentary reform.

Liverpool suffered a paralyzing stroke in 1827, which forced him to step down as prime minister. He lingered in this disabled state for a short time, dying in 1828. He was succeeded as prime minister by George Canning, who in turn was followed by Frederick John Robinson, Viscount Goderich. Canning's death and the instability of the Goderich Whig-Liberal Tory coalition, gave way to the duke of Wellington in 1828. The patrician hero of Waterloo had come to top political office at perhaps the worst possible time for a Tory of his stern cast of mind. Dissenters were demanding the repeal of their chief legal obstacle to holding public office, the Corporation Acts of 1661. Roman Catholics, likewise, were pressing the government for emancipation from their inferior constitutional position under the provisions of the Test Act of 1671. In theory, these pieces of legislation went to the heart of the British confessional state. Dissenters and Roman Catholics were excluded from local or national office unless they agreed to take communion in the Church of England, although indemnities allowed for a skirting of the law. These years of constitutional revolution laid bare the cardinal elements of English governance and demonstrated, according to Jonathan Clark, the "negative phenomenon"[4] of the severe wounding of the historical Anglican establishment; negative because one must look very hard to find in this revolution any evidence of a concerted move toward democracy. Nevertheless, to those who opposed the repeal of the Corporation Acts in 1828 and the resultant victory for Dissenters, the complete destruction of the Anglican confessional state, the religio-political compact that ensured the privileged position of the Church of England, seemed nigh.

The gloom became that much deeper for those who opposed such assumed liberality of government action when Catholic emancipation became law in 1829. "The most intractable and divisive issue in English domestic politics for the first thirty years of the nineteenth century," as Wendy Hinde calls emancipation, came to a resolution under the guiding hand of the unlikely Wellington.[5] The prime minister, like many of his fellow aristocrats, was hardly a friend of Roman Catholics, many of whom were Irish and led by the dogged and charismatic Dublin lawyer Daniel O'Connell, elected M.P. for County Clare in 1828 but unable to take his seat because of his faith. Indeed, the thought of granting emancipation to the fiery O'Connell or any other Irish Catholic struck many people in England as an unconscionable threat to both constitution and empire. The perpetually unruly Irish required the draconian imperial hand, many believed, and surely such would be supplied by Wellington's Tory government at Westminster. But practical politics and the fear of a civil breakdown in Ireland got in the way of the kind of ringing defense of the Anglican establishment so desired and expected by the partisans of the Church of England. Wellington and his home secretary, Robert Peel, rightly feared civil war in Ireland if emancipation was not granted. O'Connell himself was not a man of violence, but the same could not be said of his followers. And so, despite opposition from many Tories, including the highly influential Lord Eldon, the uncompromising leader of the Ultras, Wellington and Peel pushed Catholic emancipation through Parliament in the spring of 1829. Roman Catholics now could sit at Westminster. For defenders of the unreformed English constitution this was an outrage.[6]

Within the ancient University of Oxford the sense of outrage was especially acute. At this bastion of the Church of England, the Tories' betrayal of the Protestant constitution by allowing Catholics to sit in Parliament was seen both as treasonous and sacrilegious. It marked no less than the end of the nation as it had been since the time of Henry VIII, many feared. Peel was one of the University's two burgesses (M.P.s), and his apparent rejection of Anglican primacy was met with great anger and withering scorn by a number of college dons, especially at Oriel, an intellectual and religious hotbed at the time and home to a group of fellows whose loyalty to the Church of England was profound, as well as prickly. John Henry Newman, wiry, ascetic, brilliantly mercurial, and one of Oriel's leading fellows, quickly branded Peel a "rat" for his complicity in emancipation.[7] The insulted and perhaps chastened Peel offered to step down, an offer welcomed by Newman and other like-minded defenders of the Church of England. In the ensuing election, Sir Robert Inglis, a High Churchman and an enthusiastic antiemancipationist, was elected to Parliament. Newman's Oriel colleague and fellow traveler, the gentle John Keble, was stirred to pronounce that he was "very, very anxious that the University should do nothing which may be likely to countenance the dangerous laxity of modern politics."[8] And Hurrell Froude, yet another Oriel Fellow, red-haired and with a volcanic disposition to match, was similarly dismayed.[9] Given what would be the eventual direction of the Oxford Movement and Newman's own eventual conversion to Roman Catholicism, there is, of course, a clear irony in his concern for the Anglican establishment in its hour of need. But the road Newman would travel to Rome was a long and complicated one, and no inkling of it could be detected in 1829. In that year the Church was seen to be under attack and the only response for proper churchmen like the Oriel triumvirate was to rush to its defense.

Worse trouble for defenders of the Church lay ahead, however. In

1832, the Whig government of Lord Grey, having defeated the Tories two years earlier, introduced the Reform Bill, which altered and slightly expanded the social and demographic composition of the British electoral franchise. This expansion of the franchise, such as it was, meant very little in practical political terms—at least immediately. But after the events of 1828 and 1829, any reform of the composition of the House of Commons to allow for more middle-class members, including Protestant Dissenters, was a further blow to political tradition and the primacy of Anglicans in Parliament.

In 1833 Grey's Whigs struck yet another blow at political tradition, this time directly at the Church. The Irish Church Temporalities Bill dissolved ten redundant bishoprics and redistributed their endowments to those remaining in Ireland. The bill was defended by the government as a piece of rational legislation, which it was, but it was passed at an extremely sensitive time politically. In the midst of continued recriminations over the relationship between church and state the bill sent Newman, Keble, and Froude into paroxysms of anger. For Newman, the bill was sacrilegious and endangered the independence and integrity of the Church.[10] The state, he opined, could not be trusted to protect the Church from liberalizing influences; indeed, the state seemed to be the agent of liberalization, the unrepentant sponsor of Erastianism.

Keble responded publicly to the state's apparent transgressions by mounting the pulpit at St. Mary's, the University Church in Oxford, on July 14, 1833, and preaching a sermon that denounced England for being in a state of "national apostasy." Froude, naturally, given his lively temperament, rejoiced that Keble had called, in his view, "the Ministers Libertines and the Parliament Erastian and [implied] that the Bishops are such a set that he hardly knows whether we ought to remain in Communion with them."[11] Typically, Froude's enthusiasm was unbounded, but the sermon preached to the visiting Assize Court nevertheless proved a highly symbolic step in the beginnings of the Oxford Movement. For Newman, in hindsight, Keble's sermon indeed marked "the start of the religious movement of 1833."[12]

Newman, Keble, and Froude found themselves caught up in the events of 1829–33. These three dons from the Oriel Common Room[13] had seen the perilous direction of "revolutionary" England and were

St. Mary's, Oxford, 1857, *by Joseph Nash. Troubled by the "dangerous laxity" of modern politics in Britain, John Keble ascended the pulpit at St. Mary's on July 14, 1833, to deliver his "national apostasy" sermon. Fine Art Photographic Library Ltd / Private Collection.*

anticipating an even greater confrontation, as they saw it, with the forces of liberalism and the despoilers of the Church. But as they had come to know over the preceding few years, such an enemy lurked not only at Westminster, but could be found in the colleges of Oxford itself, especially their own.

Oriel was the most intellectually vibrant college at Oxford in the 1820s and 1830s, and the Oriel Common Room was the scene of many a spirited verbal joust. Newman became a fellow of Oriel near the outset of this period, in 1822, joining Keble, who had been there since 1811. Froude's election to a fellowship came shortly after Newman's own. Oriel's provost from 1814 to 1828, Edward Copleston, was an impressive reformist leader who turned the college into the home of many first-class honors students. Oriel was the home also of the Noetics, the self-named body of dons whose rationalism and lively debates over a range of issues were legendary within Oxford. Newman's entry into this world of blue-ribbon tutors was an unlikely one because of a nerve-wrackingly dismal performance in his final exams in 1820; he had expected a "double first" and received a mere "pass." Nevertheless, evidence of his superior intellect came through in his fellowship examination, which superseded his panicked examination performance.[14] And so the discriminating fellows of Oriel invited him to join their privileged world. Once there, the youthful and retiring Newman was overwhelmed by the brusque manner of well-established fellows such as Copleston and the aggressive, though kindly disposed, Richard Whately. Whately, a leading Noetic, was a bear of a man, and initially Newman shrank both from his physical size and his intellectual combativeness. But a mutual attraction was at work, and Whately was probably more responsible for Newman's personal and intellectual development than anyone else during his early years as an Oriel fellow. As Newman recalled later: "While I was still awkward and timid in 1822, he took me by the hand, and acted towards me the part of a gentle and encouraging instructor."[15]

Newman's affection for Whately would not last, however, because, among other reasons, as archbishop of Dublin from 1831 Whately supported the detested Irish Church bill. Keble, likewise, found Whately and the Noetics unpalatable. Keble had become a fellow of Oriel in the same year as Whately, 1811. Keble was highly intelligent, the holder of a

Oriel College, Oxford. Dating from 1326 and the epicenter of the Oxford Movement, all four of the leading Tractarians were sometime college fellows. By permission of the Provost and Fellows of Oriel College, Oxford.

double first and a clutch of prizes as an undergraduate, but he was intensely reserved. The product of a country parsonage, he disliked the kind of showy intellectualism and the less-than-humble faith that many of Oriel's fellows increasingly displayed, it seemed, in the years after his election to a fellowship. The intellectually rousing, questioning atmosphere favored by Whately was one that, Keble believed, compromised Christian faithfulness and obedience. The fact that the Oriel Common Room "stank with logic,"[16] as Newman later described it, was one of the reasons Keble decided to leave Oxford in 1823. Keble returned to rural life, settling eventually at Hursley in Hampshire, a living to which he was instituted in 1836 and where he would remain for the rest of his life.

Froude, on the other hand, could not have been less reserved in manner. He thrived on a steady diet of irony, overstatement, and denunciation. Sir George Prevost, another member of the Oriel Common

Room in those years, remembered his younger colleague this way: "Froude used to define his startling way of putting facts and arguments on the ground that it was the only way to rouse people and get their attention, and he said that when you had once done this you might modify your statements."[17] Froude's own background—he had been raised in a rural vicarage and had had a sparkling undergraduate career—was close to Keble's own. But the mix that had produced the quiet Keble resulted in a different outcome in the lively Froude.

The three young Oriel fellows gradually became close friends during the early 1820s, joined by mutual affection and a deep love for the traditions of High Church Anglicanism. Keble and Froude both came from families where high churchmanship was practiced. According to Peter Nockles, the High Churchman upheld the doctrine of the apostolic succession, was grounded in the catholic ideal of the Church, and advocated a strong establishment where the state was well aware of its divinely ordained function as the protector of the Church.[18]

Newman, conversely, had grown up in an evangelical home where the Church's tradition was much less important. The decisive feature of evangelicalism was its high subjectivity, its literal self-consciousness, and the need for each person to seek redemption from sin through the shed blood of Christ. Throughout his life Newman remembered clearly his own conversion experience at age fifteen.[19] English evangelicalism's impact on both individuals and society at this time can scarcely be overestimated. It was widely popular and probably represented "the deepest and most fervid religion in England during the first three decades of this [the nineteenth] century."[20] But Newman's years as an undergraduate had drawn him away from evangelicalism because of its disregard for baptismal regeneration, the orthodox belief in infant baptism as a soul-saving sacrament. He came to think this denial by evangelicals evidence of a wider denial of the essential mystery and wonder of God's redemptive gift. The evangelical insistence on placing the workings of regeneration under human judgment was presumptive and wrongheaded, he thought. By the mid-1820s, Newman thus had become conversant with and had accepted the main features of the High Church tradition, especially the necessary mystery and tradition of Christian faith, and his youthful evangelicalism, for the most part, had ebbed away.[21]

John Keble *(1844). Keble's popular devotional book,* The Christian Year *(1827), made him the best known of the Tractarians at the beginning of the Oxford Movement in 1833. By permission of the Warden and Fellows of Keble College, Oxford.*

John Henry Newman. *This watercolor portrait by William Ross was painted in 1845, the year of Newman's conversion to the Roman Catholic Church. Newman's brilliant intellect and rhetorical force made him the leader of the Oxford Movement. By permission of the Warden and Fellows of Keble College, Oxford.*

The Oriel threesome's shared commitment to high churchman-ship, viewed within the context of their vocation, yielded an important stake in the moral and pastoral role of the college tutor. Newman espe-cially, as an Oriel tutor from 1826, was vexed by the apparent religious laxity of many of the wealthy and aristocratic students, whose perfunc-tory appearance at chapel in order to receive communion he regarded as scandalous. Newman and Froude, after the latter's tutorial appointment in 1828, were also deeply concerned about the student practice of hiring private tutors from among recent undergraduates. They thought this practice wasteful financially and demeaning of the office and the influ-ence of college tutor and so began to lobby for substantive change in the tutorial system in 1828.

The sharp-eyed Noetic Edward Hawkins became Oriel's provost in that same year. Initially, Hawkins was receptive to the reformist ideas of Newman and his friends, who now included Robert Wilberforce, who was a son of the great abolitionist, William Wilberforce, and had been made a college tutor at the same time as Froude. But the issue of Catho-lic emancipation and Peel's stance divided the Oriel Common Room. Hawkins was on one side; Newman, Keble and Froude, on the other. College politics had become extremely divisive already, and this existing cleavage now was exacerbated by the tutorial issue.

In the spring of 1829, Newman drew up a new tutorial system that struck at what he saw as the impersonal common lecture system em-ployed by the college, which had reduced the pastoral role of the tutor and resulted in less individual attention for each student—or pupil as the term of choice was then. Equally aggravating for Newman and his friends was the allied need for paid private tuition, which pupils took advantage of whether living in or out of college. Each tutor should be responsible in the first place only for his pupils, and secondarily for those pupils of other tutors, argued Newman. In drawing up this plan New-man had the support of Oriel's senior tutor, Joseph Dornford, and of course that of Froude and Wilberforce. Critically, in what would appear to have been a small exercise in storming the ramparts, Provost Hawkins was not informed of the plan.

Eventually, in the summer of 1829, Hawkins heard about the plan, and then in October, when Michaelmas term began, made plain his disapproval of it. The provost objected to the placing of pupils under the exclusive care of one tutor, not least because it was Hawkins's responsibility to assign pupils to tutors and doing so was a difficult and delicate job depending on the personalities involved and did not need the additional complication that Newman's plan entailed.

Newman stood firm, arguing that tutoring was largely "pastoral" and that the old system of common lecturing was "incompatible with the attention to that more useful private instruction, which had imparted to the office of Tutor the importance of a clerical occupation."[22] But Hawkins remained equally resolute. By the summer of 1830 the impasse had hardened irrevocably, and Hawkins informed Newman that no more pupils would be directed his way. Newman accepted this verdict reluctantly and reverted gradually to being a fellow of the college only. So, too, did the like-minded Froude and Wilberforce.

Behind this disagreement lay more than a pedagogical issue. Hawkins was a Noetic, and his position put him on the other side of a great divide from Newman. The Noetics were dangerously liberal in the estimation of Newman, Keble, and Froude. The Church's ancient lineage and constitutional prerogatives were under threat from the critical spirit of men like Whately, Copleston, and Hawkins. "Their common disposition was to examine and criticize received beliefs in the light of history and reason," observes Bernard Reardon.[23] This iconoclastic stance clashed severely with someone of Keble's retiring temperament, for example, but precisely because of this temperament he was inclined to limit his overt opposition to Hawkins. Newman and Froude, however, were happy to attack verbally the enemies of the Church, most especially the Noetics.

Newman felt that Oriel College, which he had joined in joyous ecstasy on the day of his fellowship election, had betrayed him, in his view.[24] Oriel's Noetics were both denying the implementation of the proper kind of pastoral tuition and, much more important, attacking the independent position of the Church by their support of the Irish Church bill. Neither error could be tolerated. By the summer of 1833, Newman and his friends were prepared to do something about it beyond simply fomenting a disagreement over the style of tuition practiced at the college.

Keble's Assize sermon in mid-July may have sounded the individual trumpet of protest, but the first real gathering of like-minded defenders of the Church came at the end of that month at the rectory in Hadleigh, Suffolk, of Hugh James Rose, a fellow of Trinity College, Cambridge, and a well-respected High Churchman. The kindly Rose was sympathetic to the position of the Oriel men and opened his home as a meeting place for them. But even here, the atmosphere was not all unity and common purpose. The old High Churchmen in attendance, such as Rose and William Palmer, a fellow of Worcester College, believed the way forward lay in the time-honored practice of committees and petitions. As members of the Hackney Phalanx, named for the suburb of London in which many of the leading High Churchmen lived, they took their own party-like apparatus as the standard by which the Oxford men should operate. The younger men from Oxford held their seniors in great esteem, but on this point they declined to emulate them. Cheekily, Froude christened the old High Churchmen the "Zs" (the Oxford men were the "Xs," and the evangelicals were the "Ys" in his lexicon), and thought that the new movement would be hindered by a formulaic, channeled response to government intervention in Church affairs. Given the long parliamentary history of the Hackney Phalanx, the Tractarians' insistence on doing things their way was both risky and radical. But, officialdom would be a dead hand, Newman argued, "entangling us in a timid cautious course."[25] On principle, Newman did not attend the meeting, but for the others it put into sharp relief the fact that whatever lay ahead the unconventionality of the summer of 1833 would probably mark this protest, however long it lasted and whatever its results.

The early days of the Oxford Movement were not for the timid. Politics, both within the Church and at Westminster, were generating stirring argument and action. Indeed, as Jonathan Clark contends rightly, "The Tractarians' point of origin was more political than it was sacramental."[26] And they were soon to find that politics could be a nasty theater in which to operate. But Newman, for one, did not shy away from what might lie ahead. As he wrote to a friend in August 1833: "And how do you go on in these eventful times? Have you yet taken your part in the great battle? for surely you must soon; or are you still treating the events which pass us by as the mere scene of a theatre, the subjects of opinions, not of principles?—Surely, it is no child's play when the rights of the Church are invaded."[27]

At Hadleigh, Froude had seen firsthand the conservative mind-set of the "Zs." He expressed his concern that the zest and force with which the coming battle had to be fought might be blunted by organizational wrangling or timidity. Keble, characteristically, was much more inclined to avoid a confrontation with his seniors, but nevertheless was committed to the most effectual means of advancing the Movement. Since Keble was older than his two colleagues, and from 1831 had been Oxford's Professor of Poetry, he carried more weight in the University than either Newman or Froude did. Additionally, the publication of Keble's devotional book, *The Christian Year,* in 1827, lent a spiritual *gravitas* to him that his colleagues did not possess and no organized society could hope to deepen. But Keble could see that the formation of a society would probably have a dampening effect on the urgency and clarity of the Movement's message and so sided with Newman and Froude. As he wrote to a friend: "We do not make a formal society but only lay our heads together, as seems good to ourselves, to prepare and circulate tracts."[28]

As Keble predicted, the *Tracts for the Times* did indeed become the weapon of choice for the early years of the Movement. The early numbers were especially animated, sharp, and designed to smart. As editor of the *Tracts,* Newman sought to maintain their separate authorship and combative style. As he told Hugh James Rose: "We do not want regular troops, but sharpshooters."[29] The intended target was the so-called slumbering clergy, although Keble hoped to widen the *Tracts'* appeal and make them popular with ordinary parishioners, such as his own.[30] Newman wrote the first one, which was published on September 1, 1833. The series continued for the next eight years during which time ninety tracts were published.

The *Tracts,* especially the first thirty of them, show evidence of a deep concern by their authors for contemporary politics. Newman's pen pushes the debate along this path in the second tract, "The Catholic Church," published in early September. In it, he lambastes the Church's political masters, asking: "Did the State make us? can it unmake us? can it send out missionaries? can it arrange dioceses? Surely these are all spiritual functions. . . . No one can say that the British Legislature is in our communion or that its members are necessarily even Christians. What pretense then has it for, not merely advising, but superseding the Ecclesiastical power?"[31]

Here Newman is giving voice to the intense outrage he and his Oxford colleagues felt over the state's arrogating to itself the power to dictate to the Church changes in its sacred organizational body. The suppression of the Irish bishoprics is taken as evidence of the state's willingness to disregard the independence of the Church. The state's interventionist stance is no mere trifle, Newman argues. He rejects the proposition that "*the day is past* for stickling about ecclesiastical rights."[32] Any attempt to demean and marginalize the Oxford men's point of view means a clear attack on God's divinely inspired Church. A state that has allowed its confessionalism to fall into disuse has gone apostate; a state that is pandering to Dissenting opinion is descending into religious chaos and betraying its foundational ideal. A melange of denominations and religions is perilous for society, according to Newman, because it not only betrays the Church of England's foundation in universal Catholicism, but prepares the way for the kind of social upheaval suffered by the French for whom the destruction of the Church became an unintended article of faith during their bloody revolution.

The Church of England's central role in social control is one the Oxford men sought to maintain as well. John Keble was greatly concerned with the place of the clergy in the social order. In them lay the kind of authority and seriousness that would ensure social peace. In his view, liberalism and religious heterodoxy bred questioning and instability. In the fourth tract, published near the end of September, Keble sought to reaffirm the elevated spiritual and social position of priest. "Look on your pastor," he says, "as acting by man's commission," as the Dissenters did, "and you may respect the authority by which he acts, you may venerate and love his personal character, but it can hardly be called a *religious* veneration; there is nothing, properly, *sacred* about him. But once learn to regard him as the deputy of CHRIST, for reducing man to obedience of God; and everything about him becomes changed, everything stands in new light."[33]

The state, Keble thought, was attempting to disrupt and diminish the social usefulness and the moral power of the clergy. If successful, not only would the Church be damaged and its opponents guilty of infidelity, heresy, and schism, but society would be left on unsure footing, religio-social norms would weaken, and incivility or worse would be the result.

Froude took a different tack in his first foray into tract writing. He defended the length of the Church's services against those who would shorten them to make them more contemporary. He attacked the Protestant Reformation for introducing fundamental changes to service length and moving the Church away from its historic liturgical discipline. The tendency of Protestantism to produce schism is one outcome of a resistance to liturgical discipline based on the example of the primitive church. Without such discipline, Froude argues, schism will continue, and Church unity and social quiescence will decline.[34]

And so it went. Late in 1833, Edward Pusey, Oxford's Regius Professor of Hebrew and Canon of Christ Church Cathedral, made plain his sympathy with the Tractarians by writing a tract and attaching to it his initials. Pusey, aristocratic, formerly an Oriel fellow, and marked for a long career of leadership in the Church of England, had been slow to move in train behind the Tractarians. But now he had taken up his pen and was making public his support of their cause. In a style typical of the man, the tract was twenty-eight pages long (on the virtues of fasting, a topic of increasing personal interest), not exactly the kind of short, sharp call to action Newman had had in mind. Nevertheless, the entry of Pusey on the side of the Tractarians gave the nascent Oxford Movement "a name," in Newman's later estimation, and made it more of a force to be reckoned with.[35]

As 1834 began the Tractarians made a loud public protest against the latest transgression of the Whig government's new prime minister, Lord Melbourne, which was a bill to admit Dissenters to Oxford and Cambridge. As Church of England institutions, the two universities, or more particularly, devoted Anglicans within the two universities, had always guarded their legal position closely. At Oxford, undergraduates were required to subscribe to the Church's Thirty-nine Articles, the Church's doctrinal statement agreed upon in 1571, before enrolling; at

Edward Bouverie Pusey. *A drawing by his niece in 1853. As Regius Professor of Hebrew and Canon of Christ Church Cathedral in Oxford, as well as an aristocrat, Pusey supplied the Tractarians with a "name." Pusey House, Oxford. Photograph: M. R. Dudley.*

Cambridge, graduates were required to subscribe before being awarded their degrees. In the spring, the Tractarians published their "Oxford Declaration against the Admission of Dissenters," denouncing the Whigs' bill. The bill failed, but the fact of its introduction convinced the Tractarians of the perilous times in which they and their Church lived. Shortly thereafter, Newman came out with the *Via Media* tracts, in which he sought to explicate clearly the position of the Oxford men on the history and theology of the Church of England. In them he offered an affirmation of the Movement's commitment to the Church of England and to its position between "the (so called) Reformers and the Romanists,"[36] and scotching the criticisms that were beginning to be made over the Tractarians' apparent attraction to all things Roman Catholic.

John Bowden, Newman's best friend from his undergraduate days at Trinity College, had become greatly concerned with the Tractarians' apparent closeness to Roman Catholicism and warned Newman that the charge of "rank Popery" was not far off unless the Tractarians moderated their tone. Newman responded with the *Via Media* tracts, which for the time being, clarified and secured the Oxford Movement's position within the bosom of the Church.[37]

But in the reforming atmosphere of the time the traditional Church of England was on the cusp of deep structural change at the behest of both politicians and many clergy. Severe ecclesiastical abuses of one sort or another, especially simony, the holding of multiple livings, had dogged the Church since the eighteenth century. Industrialization and urbanization presented new challenges with which the Church seemed unable to cope and drove reformers to advocate wholesale change in the way the Church performed its various tasks.[38] The Whig government had responded to these concerns in 1832 by forming a committee (the "Ecclesiastical Commission") to investigate the workings of the Church and to recommend ways in which they might be improved. Naturally, the Oxford men denounced the Commission, arguing that it represented yet another example of state interference in the sacred affairs of the Church.

Similarly, the Tractarians attacked the attempt in 1835 by the Heads of Houses at Oxford, the university's administrative body, to throw out the requirement that undergraduates subscribe to the Thirty-nine Articles. This liberalizing measure, sponsored by the Whigs at Westminster and the Noetics at Oriel, was voted on and defeated in May by Convocation. Its defeat was in large part caused by the contempt shown it by Newman, Keble, and Froude. In the 1835 tract "Church and State," Froude made clear his own and his colleagues' hatred of the state's meddling. Froude, who was suffering now from tuberculosis and within a year of an early death, wrote with his customary fury that "we are naturally jealous of the attempts that are making to disunite, as it is called, Church and State; which in fact means neither more nor less, in the mouths of those who clamour for it, than a general confiscation of Church property, and a repeal of the few remaining laws which make the true Church the Church of England."[39]

The apparent constitutional revolution had "so entirely altered" the relations between church and state, contended Froude, that the state demonstrated now a "disgraceful negligence about our most sacred interests."[40] Froude was willing to go further than his colleagues in his condemnation of the established Church and the so-called error-filled Protestantism that undergirded it. Perhaps this was because he had started from a more extreme position than his friends; more likely it was because facing imminent death he had nothing to lose. And in Froude's aptly titled *Remains,* his private journals edited anonymously by Newman and Keble and published posthumously in 1838, the dead man was unsparing in his denunciation from beyond the grave of the Protestant Reformation and the established Church of England. Once Froude's inflammatory words were in the public realm, the firestorm was unstoppable.

Back in 1835, however, Froude's declaration of the Tractarians' political position was dangerously radical, showing a deep animosity toward the state and a refusal to tolerate its intrusions into the proper realm of the Church. Newman and Keble were equally vexed by the arrogance, ignorance, and insensitivity displayed by the state as embodied by Melbourne and the Whigs. Melbourne's indifference toward all things religious and his puzzlement at theological divisions were well known. The Tractarians, perhaps, were the most puzzling of all to the prime minister, as his comments to Lord Holland, even less well-disposed to religious matters than Melbourne himself and whose London house was the center of Whig political and literary society, display: "I hardly make out what Puseyism [using one of the pejorative terms for the Oxford Movement which had been attached to it following the publication of Pusey's tract] is. Either I am dull, or its apostles are very obscure. I have got one of their chief Newman's publications with an appendix of four hundred and forty-four pages. I have read fifty-seven and cannot say I understand a sentence, or any idea whatever."[41] As far as the Tractarians were concerned, such an admission merely confirmed the obvious Erastianism, if not the apostasy, of the leader of His Majesty's Government.

In light of such Whig depredations, Froude explicitly condemned establishment and called for the Church of England to save itself by escaping from the more and more irreligious hand of the state. Newman's inclinations in this direction increased in the mid-late 1830s, too, but did not reach their logical end until the early 1840s. Of course, neither Keble nor Pusey, both overwhelmingly committed to the Church of England whatever its failings, ever reached this conclusion, although it was thought by many in both the Church and the public that Pusey, the "hermit of Christ Church," was destined for Rome.

As we have seen, the *Tracts for the Times* was one way in which the Tractarians were able to spread their political gospel; the *British Critic* became another. The *Critic* began life in 1793 as a High Church publication in opposition to the anticlericalism of the French Revolution. Joshua Watson and Henry Handley Norris, two prominent members of the Hackney Phalanx, purchased the magazine in 1814. In its early years, the *Critic* was a general-interest literary organ reflective of its time in reporting "all worthwhile publications in all fields of knowledge."[42] But in the overheated atmosphere of the war years the magazine's religious pedigree became more prominent, especially under the ownership of the devout Watson and Norris. Later, in the 1830s, the *Critic* evolved into a voice for the Oxford men, and in 1838 Newman became its editor.

For Newman, the English confessional state was gradually proving itself a cause almost beyond redemption, and as editor he ensured that the *Critic* made clear this sad state of affairs. Accordingly, he excluded moderate churchmen, such as Samuel Wilberforce, another son of William Wilberforce and later bishop of Oxford, from the pages of the magazine on the grounds that the Church-state unity they espoused was mere Erastianism made more acceptable by earnest appeals to Bishop Richard Hooker, the sixteenth-century Anglican divine whose writings were most often used to uphold the establishment.[43] Even the strong churchman and rising Tory politician William Gladstone was no match for Newman's considered stance. Gladstone's tortuous attempt to offer a sustainable theory of church and state in his 1838 book, *The State in Its Relations with the Church,* failed to impress both Newman and, for that matter, the more tolerant Keble, as we shall see in Chapter 4.

Newman edited the *Critic* for almost three years, from July 1838 until April 1841. He controlled the magazine and took it at a steady pace away from its High Church base toward a more overt sympathy for Rome. Naturally, this move angered the old High Churchmen, the so-called Zs, who saw their traditional magazine being taken from them and used for the increasingly suspicious purposes of the increasingly suspicious Tractarians. Newman continued to advocate Church independence, harking back to the Fathers of the Church as the foundation upon which the contemporary Church must be built. This "patristic fundamentalism,"[44] as Peter Nockles calls it perceptively, was the Tractarians' bulwark against what they saw as the vagaries of ecclesiastical and secular politics and the errors of religious denominationalism.

In the spring of 1839, Thomas Mozley, fellow of Oriel, future brother-in-law of Newman, and young lion of the Movement, made a contribution to the *Critic* that offered a kind of summation of the Tractarians' position on church and state. In a review of Edward King's orthodox book *Church and King* (1837), Mozley concluded by asserting that "a consecrated kingdom [has] ceased to be."[45] The state had betrayed the Church and was irredeemable. Attempts to revive such a unity were pointless, Mozley contended, because church and state are joined in a false and, for the Church, degrading union. The faster the Church extricated itself from its position in the establishment, the better. All who opposed this view, especially the old High Churchmen, were in error. "If establishmentism were Christianity," Mozley wrote sarcastically, "the country might with a little forcing soon be filled with good Christians."[46] But Mozley looked on the antidisestablishmentarians with contempt. The establishment was beyond reclamation, in his view, and the

Church must revivify itself based on a renewed commitment to catholic independence.

Newman left the editor's chair at the *Critic* in 1841. By then he was moving irrevocably along the road to conversion. As Newman saw it, his work at the magazine was finished because he and his colleagues had said everything that they needed to say to articulate fully their position on church and state. In the great arena of national politics, the Tractarians had found the state almost completely unable to act as the guardian of the Church and were now, it seemed, ready to abandon wholly the old verities of the English constitution. Keble and Pusey resisted this radical stance, but the political initiative of the Movement was now beginning to pass to other, younger and more extreme men such as Mozley, W. G. Ward, and Frederick Oakeley, who took their lead from the radical Newman, who had assumed the unofficial leadership of the Movement. Newman, by this point in despair over his fundamental beliefs, was on the verge of beginning his retreat from Oriel, from the Movement, from the Church of England altogether. In 1843, he retired to the village of Littlemore on the outskirts of Oxford and remained there until the famous rainy night in October 1845 when he was received into the Roman Catholic Church by the itinerant Passionist priest, Father Dominic Barberi. And by that point, Rome's latest and most celebrated English convert had abandoned all interest in politics.

But even though national politics may have been of little importance to the reclusive and intensely contemplative Newman of the early to mid-1840s, the Movement's initial political concentration on the issues of church and state had drawn in professional politicians whose sympathies, unlike the irreligious Melbourne's, lay with the Movement. Chief among these politicians were Gladstone, whom we encountered earlier with his long treatise on church and state, and Benjamin Disraeli, the young Conservative trying desperately to rise in the Party while under the thumb of ex-Oxford burgess and indisposed party leader and prime minister, Sir Robert Peel.

Gladstone was early attracted to the regenerative thrust of the Movement, becoming in the late 1830s a member of the Additional Curates Society, which sought to place curates who espoused High Church and Tractarian principles in needy populous parishes, and then later helping to organize the Engagement, a lay Tractarian brotherhood of parliamentarians committed to doing good works. As with most features of his life, especially the religious, Gladstone was excruciatingly serious about the Movement and sought to ensure that its charted course remained in the best interests of the Church. He corresponded with all the leading members of the Movement and in 1845 wrote to Newman in a desperate, and of course fruitless, attempt to try and dissuade him from defecting from the Church of England.

The theory of government and establishment Christianity Gladstone articulated in his treatise *State and Church* was one that exalted the Church, ascribing to it the role of society's main regenerative agent. The state was likewise raised high and seen as a moral actor in the Aristotelian sense where the civil power is accorded a conscience. Gladstone believed in the organic unity of church and state: "The highest duty and highest interest of a body politic alike tend to place it in close relations of cooperation with the Church of Christ," wrote Gladstone.[47] This ideal, however, was one that could not be realized in early Victorian England, as Gladstone came to acknowledge sadly. He never gave up on the ideal of organic unity,[48] but by the early 1840s the "conditions of the age,"[49] as he called emergent pluralism and secularization, precluded such idealism. Parliament's tasks did not include "evangelisation" in order to restore the catholic ethos of the Church of England, he concluded. Gladstone recognized the inexorability of Parliament's and the country's pluralism and secularization, though he did not endorse them.

For Gladstone, the Oxford Movement was a profoundly serious attempt to recall the Church of England to its apostolic and ecclesiastic roots. But because of the Movement's increasingly Romanist and dogmatic bent, it clashed with Gladstone's pragmatic governmental responsibilities and sympathies. He was devoted entirely to the Church of England, whatever its state of health, and although keenly aware of the Church's shortcomings never flirted with the idea of throwing it over for Rome. Membership in the national church was the pivot of Gladstone's existence and helps to explain, as Agatha Ramm and Perry Butler have pointed out, why Gladstone always resisted Tractarian extremes and can be called a member of the Movement only if such a caveat is first recognized.[50]

Ultimately, Gladstone saw the Oxford Movement as a way to combat religious apathy and to stimulate a new appreciation of the long history of the Church of England and its foundation in Catholic Christianity. But a Newman-led Movement could not sustain a theory of church and state that satisfied Gladstone; and therefore, to him its political importance never surpassed its personal religious value.

For the worldly Disraeli, conversely and not surprisingly, the Oxford Movement's influence was felt most keenly in party politics. In the early to mid-1840s Disraeli was at the helm of Young England, a coterie of youthful Conservative M.P.s who were frustrated at their lack of influence in Peel's government and wished to make their mark by championing a brand of Tory politics different from the politics of brokering a peace between advocates of industry and supporters of the Corn Laws practiced by their chief. As Robert Blake observes, "Young England . . . beckon[ed] to those incurable romantics for whom political life is something more than a humdrum profession."[51] Romanticism was Young England's lodestar.

Disraeli and his fellow Young Englanders—George Smythe, Lord John Manners, and Alexander Baillie-Cochrane—also reflected the impact that medievalism had on early Victorian England. Their own medievalism manifested itself most clearly in the advocacy of an organic view of history in which the past was held in great reverence, church and state were closely entwined politically, and the Church was the social anchor of society.

Disraeli, as the senior and most ambitious member of Young England, had the most to gain should it be successful in vaulting the quartet of backbenchers nearer the top of the Conservative Party's greasy pole. Disraeli's views on the place of the Church put Young England firmly within the web of the Oxford Movement, and Blake characteristically is direct and right about the linkage: "Young England was the Oxford Movement translated . . . from religion into politics."[52]

Disraeli's mild success as a writer of popular novels in the 1820s and 1830s led him to pen three important and serious works—his political trilogy—in the 1840s. Two of these books, *Coningsby* (1844) and *Sybil* (1845), were manifestos of Young England's position on political and social affairs. The Oxford Movement's insistence on the centrality of the

Church to the well-being of the country is captured well by Disraeli's injunction in *Coningsby:* "It is by the Church . . . and by the Church alone that I see any chance of regenerating the national character."[53] Disraeli's subsequent demand that the Church must be run on its "real principles"[54] reflects the Oxford Movement's call for a renewed understanding and acceptance of apostolicity and the rejection of the comfortable Erastianism practiced by many Anglicans in Parliament and parish alike.

In *Sybil*, Disraeli examines closely the dismal social conditions generated by industrial England and meditates on what a missionary Church and a rejuvenated aristocracy might do to ameliorate the worst of them. In the fictional figure of Aubrey St. Lys, Disraeli creates an Anglican cleric who is moved greatly by the squalor he sees around him in the city of Mowbray (Manchester) and disputes with the local factory owner over the wages and living standards of his workers. As Charles Egremont, Disraeli's protagonist, says of him: "St. Lys thinks it is his duty to enter all societies. That is the reason why he goes to Mowbray Castle, as well as to the squalid courts and cellars of the town. He takes care that those who are clad in purple and fine linen shall know the state of their neighbours."[55]

Disraeli modeled St. Lys on Frederick Faber, an early Tractarian and an erstwhile fellow of University College, Oxford, who moved to the Lake District, there to fall under the sway of the poet William Wordsworth and to dream of a revival of the old England of perceived organic unity. Disraeli takes the ethereal characteristics of Faber, makes them practical in the figure of St. Lys, who then brings them to bear on the irreligious laborers of Mowbray, the "hundred thousand heathens" in need of a Church that really cares about their plight.[56]

Eventually, Faber would convert to Roman Catholicism, an outcome Disraeli did not wish for any of the Tractarians because of his ultimate commitment to the Church as established. Nonetheless, the Tractarians' devotion to a renewed Church of England, steeped in historic catholic tradition, was reason enough for Disraeli to endorse their mission and to take from it what he could for the benefit of Young England.

As a movement primarily of the heart and of the imagination, Young England's practical political success was negligible. By the mid-

1840s Young England had burned itself out. Like the Tory Party itself, the group ruptured over the Maynooth bill, Peel's plan to make the Catholic seminary in Ireland the recipient of a permanent, rather than an annual, government subsidy. Disraeli voted against the bill, while Smythe and Manners voted for it at the alarmed insistence of their Peel-supporting fathers (Baillie-Cochrane was ill and not in attendance in the House). There is a small amount of irony in Disraeli's refusal to support a bill designed to place a Catholic seminary on surer financial footing, although his establishmentarianism cannot be doubted. Was not the old faith, of course clothed in Anglican garb, at the core of Young England's blueprint for national restoration? In any event, Young England petered out in 1846, but not before it had made its mark as the political analogue of the Oxford Movement. Its brief popularity made the Oxford Movement's necessarily more religious message more accessible than it was otherwise, though Disraeli was always careful to steer clear of a personal alignment with the Tractarians. The No Popery! brush smeared widely in anti-Catholic England, and Disraeli did well to stay out of its way. For Disraeli, the future lay in consolidating his position in a Conservative Party without Peel at the helm. And when Peel died in 1850, the one-time Young Englander got his chance to rise high.[57]

In R. W. Church's classic account, *The Oxford Movement: Twelve Years, 1833–1845,* first published over a century ago, the Anglican revival ends with Newman's much-lamented going over to Rome. Indeed, Church's final chapter is entitled simply and sadly, "The Catastrophe." Newman's departure from the Church of England is seen by Church as the last act of the Oxford Movement after which the Tractarians lost their leader and spiritual guide and the Movement ceased to be. In a restricted sense the Oxford Movement did end in 1845. But the significant changes brought to Anglicanism by the Tractarians were of course not canceled by Newman's departure for Rome. During the middle and later years of the nineteenth century, Anglo-Catholicism—the heir to the Oxford Movement—came to encapsulate many of the ideas and practices advocated by the Tractarians: reverence for the early church, clerical vestments, high altars, solemn masses, and religious statuary. From his canon's stall at Christ Church Cathedral, Oxford, Dr. Pusey was the visible head of Anglo-Catholicism, although he always rejected a leadership role and the idea of Church parties altogether, but not convincingly.[58] Nonetheless, Pusey's direct link to the Movement's storied years gave him special weight in matters both ecclesiastical and religious. Newman's conversion and longtime residence at the Oratory in Birmingham and Keble's voluntary seclusion at Hursley left Pusey as the last leading representative of the Movement in Oxford. And thus it was to him that Anglo-Catholics looked for guidance and support. Politically, issues of church and state remained important and contested for most of the nineteenth century, and Pusey was the chief spokesperson for the catholic party within the Church of England.

The Oxford Movement generated much controversy in the 1830s and 1840s because it emerged in the midst of far-reaching changes to the state that opponents feared would alter forever the place of the Church within the establishment. This intense period of reform naturally ran its course, but this did not mean that the issues raised and the battles fought brought to an end the overarching concern of many Anglicans: the place of the Church in modern British society. For the remainder of the nineteenth century, beginning with the Gorham controversy over baptismal regeneration in 1850, Anglo-Catholics carried the ideas of the Oxford Movement into the public realm in an effort to ensure that catholic doctrine was not ignored whenever ecclesiastical decisions were made. Whether successful or not in arguing their case, Anglo-Catholics, under the reluctant leadership of Pusey, were an important presence in religio-political affairs.

One such affair emerged in the late 1840s. In 1847, the Tractarians' old enemy, Renn Dickson Hampden, a former Oriel fellow, Noetic, and Regius Professor of Divinity at Oxford, was elevated to the see of Hereford. The newly enthroned Hampden had borne the brunt of a vigorous attack launched by Newman back in 1836 over his alleged liberalism. Four years prior to that in 1832, Hampden had delivered the important Bampton Lectures at Oxford in which he questioned the religious soundness of technical, credal theology. Then, in 1836, the well-organized and combative Tractarians decided to launch a protest against Hampden based on their devotion to religious dogma, such as that found in the creeds of the Church of England. That same year the Regius Professorship of Divinity came open, and much to the surprise and dismay of the Tractarians, Melbourne, the prime minister, did the unthinkable, even for a Whig, and appointed Hampden to the chair. The Tractarians reacted with fury, launching strongly worded petitions to an unimpressed Melbourne and to an uninterested King William IV. Newman quickly wrote a pointed rebuttal to Hampden's four-year-old Bampton Lectures, the *Elucidations of Dr Hampden's Theological Statements*. All this activity resulted in Oxford's Convocation passing a statute rebuking Hampden: "He hath in his published writings so treated matters theological that the University hath no confidence in him."[59] Much to the Tractarians horror, Hampden's appointment stood nonetheless.

Now, in 1847, Pusey and others objected vigorously when the new prime minister, Lord John Russell, appointed Hampden to the episcopacy. Pusey was greatly dismayed to see the state override the expressed position of bishops and prominent clergy and their representation of the Church at large, but it was the soon-to-follow Gorham judgment which put the issue into sharpest relief for the post-Tractarian generation.

In 1847, also, the High Church bishop of Exeter, Henry Phillpotts, refused to institute the Reverend George Gorham to the living of Bramford Speke in the diocese of Exeter. Phillpotts's refusal was based on what he deemed to be Gorham's heterodox views on baptismal regeneration, an issue of seeming unending controversy, which divided Anglo-Catholics and evangelicals. Eventually, Gorham appealed his diocesan's decision to the highest level, the Judicial Committee of the Privy Council, where it was upheld in 1850. Gorham was then instituted to his living by the archbishop of Canterbury.

Pusey and former Tractarians, such as James Hope and Henry Manning, were outraged by the decision. In July 1850, an enormous churchmen's rally was held in London at which Pusey denounced the government for its abuse of the civil power in once again violating the Church's sacred domain. As he exclaimed to the assembled multitude: "We stand . . . where two roads part, the way of the world and the way of the Church. . . . For if the state will not, as Magna Carta pledges it, allow that 'the Church should have liberties inviolate,' we must ask that the state will set us free from itself."[60] Although Pusey did not really advocate disestablishment, he was ready at least to call for it for rhetorical effect. The Gorham judgment had a deeper effect on others, however, the most notable being Henry Manning, who would shortly follow in Newman's footsteps to Rome.

The Gorham case cast a long shadow over church-state relations.

For the balance of the century Anglo-Catholics took refuge from Erastian encroachment by a continuous resistance based on a scholarly defense of and a historical reverence for Church tradition and authority. Within the Church of England, too, some took refuge from the evangelicals and the Broad Churchmen—as the liberals were now known—in staking out the ground of highly ritualistic worship. Initially, Pusey was not among them because his interest in ritualism was minimal; his concerns were overwhelmingly doctrinal and spiritual. But as Anglo-Catholicism's nominal leader he believed ritualism had a place as the outward expression of inner devotion. Moreover, he was convinced that ritualism was grounded in a lay interest and was not, in the main, being foisted upon unreceptive parishioners by a controlling priesthood.[61]

Politically, the ritualism issue climaxed in 1874 when the Conservative government of Disraeli, now long past his Young England days and indisposed to politically difficult manifestations of the "old faith," introduced the Public Worship Regulation Bill. Many "Protestant" parishioners had become increasingly restive about the "Catholic" practices of their clergy, sometimes to the point of open rebellion and the destruction of Church property. In response, Disraeli, with the parliamentary support of the staunchly evangelical Lord Shaftesbury, introduced legislation designed to curb ritualism, and indeed some clergymen were prosecuted under its terms. Publicly, Pusey objected to the government's course of action. Privately, he hoped that the ritualists would cease in what he thought were their needless provocations, the result of which had been yet another unwelcome intrusion of the long arm of the state into Church affairs.

In the last years before his death in 1882, Pusey relaxed his stern view of ritualism, finally acknowledging in it the true hand of Tractarianism. But his declining years in Oxford were troubled also by the ending of the monopoly in 1871 that Anglicans had over college fellowships and offices. Mandatory subscription to the Thirty-nine Articles had been done away with for undergraduates in the mid-1850s, much to Pusey's and Keble's dismay. Though remaining very much Anglican in culture and ethos, the ancient universities of Oxford and Cambridge were no longer confessionally exclusive Church of England institutions by law.

Pusey's and Keble's unimpeachable commitment to the establish-

ment meant that the Anglo-Catholic party never abandoned the church
and state ideal in the middle to late nineteenth century. Both men believed profoundly in the sacral idea of kingship and the necessity of a
proper understanding of the tutelary role of the monarch. Religious feeling must lie behind political values, they believed. Disestablishment,
which Radicals were calling for with considerable insistence in the latter
years of the Victorian era, would have been disastrous as far as Pusey
and Keble were concerned because national politics would have been
desacralized entirely. Equally for them, the abandonment of the state by
the Church was full of peril because it would have meant an irreplaceable
loss of "our ancient institutions and our collegiate and parochial
churches; the churches wherein our fathers have worshipped from generation to generation; the representatives of those wherein God was first
worshipped here," Pusey opined.[62]

For the Tractarians in their formative years, politics meant primarily the chain of issues found in the phrase, church and state. At the
outset of the Oxford Movement, the hand of the state was seen as especially invasive and onerous by the more radical members, such as Froude
and Mozley. Newman gradually became more and more radicalized
throughout the 1830s, whereas Keble and Pusey never lost sight of the
necessity, in their view, of retaining the church-state union. National
and university politics were never mere sport for the Tractarians, as they
seemed to be for their Whig enemies, but turned always on the cardinal
question of the proper relationship between church and state. Froude
died before he could answer fully the question; Newman found his answer in Rome; Keble and Pusey found it in a continuous and lifelong
struggle to defend the establishment, but without compromising the position of the Church. As Keble said at the time of the Gorham case: "If
the Church of England were to fail, it should be found in my parish."[63]
But there was no chance of that at Hursley. Unfortunately for Keble,
however, the Church of England was now to be found mostly in places
unlike his sylvan Hursley retreat and, because of that, appeared to have
failed already.

2 Religion & Theology
PRINCIPLES AND PROMULGATION

*E*ven though politics in the form of the controversy over the Irish Church Temporalities Bill sparked the beginning of the Oxford Movement in 1833, it is to religion and theology that one must turn in order to apprehend the forces which undergirded the Movement. The Oxford Movement's impact on the religion and theology of the Church of England was immense and profound. In order to give their critique a sense of urgency, the Tractarians charged the eighteenth-century Church with corruption and somnolence.[1] This view was rebutted strongly at the time by High Churchmen, and in work done recently by Nigel Yates the Tractarians have been shown to have painted with far too broad a brush in this regard.[2] Still, the men of Oxford believed that Anglican religious practice had been debased by Erastianism—the doctrine of the supremacy of the state over the church in ecclesiastical matters—and liberalism, and only through a concerted attempt at reviving the Church of England's lost patristic heritage would the contemporary Church be able to redeem itself. The idea of the Church's decay pervaded their thinking, and it was used as a starting point for their task of revival.[3]

The roots of the Oxford Movement lie in the high view of the Church adopted by Newman as a young man in the 1820s, and held always in one form or another by Keble, Pusey, and Froude. The corporate Church was God's sacred instrument on earth, the Oxford men believed fervently, and their deepening understanding of this idea is what lay at the center of their apprehension of the Church of England's compromised position as a religious body in the early years of the nineteenth century.

This chapter will probe the religion and theology of the Oxford Movement. What did the men of the Movement consider to be the proper Anglican stance? What did they see as deficient in Anglican religion and theology as it stood in the first half of the nineteenth century? What was their interpretation of the nature of the Church of England's catholic heritage, and how could it be revived? How did Tractarianism influence Anglican religion and theology during the cardinal 1833–45 period especially, as well as afterward?

Religion was the lifeblood of the Oxford men, and the more *real* they could make it, for themselves and for others, the closer they would come to meeting their goal of Church revival. As Newman recalled in his memoir, *Apologia Pro Vita Sua,* "two and two only absolute and luminously self-evident beings, myself and my creator," animated his life.[4] The closer that Anglican religion and theology could be brought to a recognition of this stated reality, the truer such Anglicanism would be.

The High Church tradition of the Church of England is the starting point for any investigation of the religion and theology of the Oxford Movement. In recent years much work has been done to illuminate the history of eighteenth- and nineteenth-century high churchmanship, especially that of Peter Nockles and Kenneth Hylson-Smith.[5] In Chapter 1 we examined closely the political features of high churchmanship; here, the focus is on their religion and theology. What did High Churchmen believe, and why, and how did they influence the Tractarians?

In the pre-Tractarian era, a "High Churchman in the Church of England," states Nockles in a carefully nuanced definition,

> tended to uphold in some form the doctrine of apostolical succession as a manifestation of his strong attachment to the Church's catholicity and apostolicity as a branch of the universal church catholic. . . . He believed in the supremacy of Holy Scripture and set

varying degrees of value on the testimony of author-
ised standards such as the Creeds, the Prayer Book,
and the Catechism. He valued the writings of the early
Fathers. . . . He upheld in a qualified way the primacy
of dogma and laid emphasis on the doctrine of baptismal grace, both in the eucharist and in baptism. . . .
He tended to cultivate a practical spirituality based on
good works nourished by sacramental grace and exemplified in acts of self-denial and charity rather than on
any subjective conversion experience or unruly pre-
tended manifestations of the Holy Spirit.[6]

For the Oxford men the High Church tradition became both a
door through which catholic practice could be apprehended, and a bar-
rier to the independence of the Church they came gradually to demand.
The Hackney Phalanx, sometimes called the Clapton Sect in contradis-
tinction to the evangelical Clapham Sect, that group of churchmen
whose shared London address gave a name to their common beliefs,
were the inheritors of the catholic tradition within the Church of England stemming from the period of the English Reformation. In the
twenty years leading up to the Oxford Movement High Churchmen
exerted considerable influence on Church affairs, especially on ecclesiastical preferment based on their commitment to defending the formulas
of the Church from attacks on them by Dissenters. The influential High
Churchman Henry Handley Norris, rector of South Hackney, was popularly known as the "bishop-maker" for his influence on Lord Liverpool
during his fifteen years as prime minister (1812–27).[7] More important
still was Joshua Watson, whom we will examine in detail presently and
who was central to the existence of the Hackney Phalanx.

There were many strands within High Church religion, a faith
epitomized by the Hackney Phalanx, which were especially attractive to
the Tractarians in their formative period. The example of antiquity provided a vitally important one. The writings of the early Fathers were
looked upon as the basis for sound churchmanship, as exemplified in the
primitive church. In the early part of the nineteenth century many edi-
tions of the works of the Fathers and commentaries on these works were

published. Patristic theology received a public forum through its usual airing in the annual Bampton Lectures at Oxford. The Tractarians found much that appealed to them in the history of apostolicity and its championing by High Churchmen, and it spurred them to publish a *Library of the Fathers* in 1836.

For the Tractarians, antiquity became bedrock, the unquestioned locus of authority within the Church. By the late 1830s, this fundamentalist stance gradually became stronger, diverging clearly from that held by old High Churchmen, whose own view of antiquity was a more limited one.[8] For High Churchmen, antiquity was elastic. The early church and the Fathers provided a reference point against which to test the Protestant inheritance of the events of the English Reformation and the writings of the Caroline divines. Most important in this regard was the work of the sixteenth-century Church of England theologian Richard Hooker, author of the immensely influential *Laws of Ecclesiastical Polity* (1594–97), whose writings lay at the intellectual heart of the establishment. The Tractarians, on the other hand, idealized a Church grounded in the unaltered and unblemished precepts of the church fathers and without mediation. For Newman in particular, the High Church predilection for a restricted view of antiquity—and therefore in his estimation a restricted view of what was essential to the faith—became unacceptable. He expressed this position in his *Lectures on the Prophetical Office* (1837), where he sought to formulate "a correct theory" of the Church by asserting the necessity of the full acceptance of its ancient heritage.

Naturally, therefore, Newman exhibited considerable impatience with the old High Churchmen and their stubborn attachment—in his view—to traditional orthodoxy. Hugh James Rose, a prominent member of the school and an early supporter of the Oxford Movement, attempted to warn Newman about the perils of accepting the norms of antiquity uncritically: "All that is in Antiquity is not good; and much that was good for Antiquity would not be good for us."[9] But Newman did not wish to hear dissent from a "Z" (to recall Froude's nickname for the old High Churchmen of Rose's type), and so he continued to push at the strictures imposed by a tradition he was no longer willing to accept as normative or binding.[10]

While the struggle was joined at this higher level, there remained much else lower down the scale where the Tractarians and the High Churchmen intersected agreeably. A rigid insistence on the divine basis of the threefold ministerial order: bishop, priest, and deacon was an inheritance the Tractarians welcomed, as was the episcopal system of church government and the apostolic succession. In none of these areas was there absolute harmony between the Tractarians and the old High Churchmen, but there was at least sufficient commonality to keep the parties tolerant of one another until the rupture brought on by the publication of Froude's *Remains* in 1837–38, and *Tract* no. 90 in 1841.

Catholicity, however, was at the heart of the Tractarian project, and their proprietary interest in it served to anger High Churchmen whose devotion to the catholic principle—as they understood it—was no less fierce than that of the Oxford men. The High Church conception of catholicity was based on the understanding of the Church of England as a branch of the universal church, upholding the ancient catholic faith and the apostolic succession. Its leading theorist was Charles Daubeny, an early member of the Hackney Phalanx, and from his pen flowed much that became religious orthodoxy in the minds of his fellow High Churchmen. "Every Christian society," he wrote, "possessing the characteristic marks of the Church of Christ, I consider to be a separate branch of the Catholic or Universal visible Church upon Earth."[11] In *Guide to the Church* (1798) Daubeny argued forcefully that in order for a church to be true it must display the mark of an ordained ministry whose authority came through the apostolic succession. Thus the Church of England, the Church of Ireland, as well as other episcopal churches, could claim rightfully to be truly catholic based on their adherence to the apostolic ideal.

While High Churchmen disputed Rome's claim to exclusive catholicity, they were equally as disparaging of Protestant Dissent's claims of truth, which were based not on membership in the visible church catholic but rather on the invisible church of believers. Schism was intolerable to High Churchmen, and they routinely denounced the various Protestant sectarian bodies for the damage they inflicted willfully on the universal church. As one enraged High Churchman put it, the schismatical mind of Dissenters made them deserve "the severity of hell torments."[12] In this kind of hearty condemnation of Dissenters the old High Churchmen and the Tractarians were in fundamental agreement.

So, too, were they in agreement originally over Rome. As we shall see in the next chapter in our account of Newman and Froude's Mediterranean journey of 1833, the Tractarians, like so many of their coreligionists and countrymen at large, initially thought Roman Catholicism to be irrevocably error-filled. Whether such errors were the popularly held ones of papal authority and "priestcraft," or deeper objections to Roman Catholic theology and practice, Rome had corrupted the church and therefore had no legitimate claim to universality, it was believed. Anti-Catholicism was an elixir that sustained much of the British populace in the early to mid-nineteenth century, and there was a considerable amount of it among both High Churchmen and Tractarians.[13] But unlike the wider public whose discrimination against Rome was often crude and based on racial and religious stereotypes, the anti-Catholicism of High Churchmen and Tractarians rested on a defense of the rightness and the necessity of the English Protestant Reformation during which the whole Church of England had made a public protest against Rome. They believed Anglican doctrine to be true, not merely expedient, as Jonathan Clark points out.[14] The Church of England, as a branch church, was a doctrinally sound expression of the church catholic and remained so even though it had made a judgment against Rome. No other grounds were necessary for it to claim catholic membership. Popular anti-Catholicism rested on a demonization of Rome and the worldwide apparatus of its church; nothing of the sort was needed by High Churchmen and Tractarians in order to denounce Rome. Roman error was fundamental, they believed. The Church of England, on the other hand, was both catholic and "well-earthed." Nothing Rome could say or do, they believed, could change these evident facts.

Indeed, some High Churchmen argued that in breaking with Rome the Church of England was returning to its own roots, to "her primitive character," in the words of Thomas Burgess, the High Church bishop of St. David's.[15] It is important, however, that not all High Churchmen agreed with this "origins" argument. Some called for an eventual reunion of the Roman and English Churches, and it was this strain of thinking which would influence most closely the more catholic-minded Tractarians, especially Newman.

But Newman's antipathy to Rome took a long time to die. His endorsement of Anglican ecclesiology remained fairly firm through the mid-1830s. But it began to weaken in tandem with his loss of faith in the establishment. He rejected publicly the idea of the Church of England as a "branch" of the church universal in *Tract* no. 71, published in 1836.[16] Controversy with the Romanists had overtaken the Church of England "like a summer's cloud," opined Newman, and at the root of it was the Church's unwillingness to state formally what it believed. He blamed the "protection and favour" accorded the Church by the state for this ecclesiological laxity, and predicted that the truth lay somewhere "between the two contending parties," Canterbury and Rome.[17] As we know, Newman's lukewarm endorsement of the Church of England's position, its "incompleteness in our own system,"[18] as he described it, was beginning to alienate some High Churchmen. They detected rightly a move by Newman away from the Church of England in search of a theory of the whole Church, not merely the marks of one that had satisfied Daubeny and those who accepted his teaching. Of course, Newman's struggle would not be resolved until 1845. In the meantime, the Tractarians continued to develop their middle road—their enunciation of the proper Anglican stance—their *via media*. And it was done in part through the High Church literary organ, the *British Critic,* introduced in Chapter 1.

The *British Critic* dated from 1793. It was founded in order to bolster the cardinal institutions of Britain in the face of the French Revolution's attack on monarchical and social tradition. In 1814, the *Critic* was purchased by the resolute High Churchmen Joshua Watson and Henry Norris. Together they strengthened its conservative bias, of which a staunch high churchmanship formed a considerable part. Beginning in 1826 an even greater religious earnestness was exhibited in the pages of the *Critic* when it merged with the similarly positioned *Quarterly Theological Review and Ecclesiastical Record.* During this time the editorial character of the *Critic* appealed directly to a High Church readership of considerable size.[19] Despite their internecine religious differences, High Churchmen had an essentially common cultural outlook, which they

came to depend upon the *Critic* to represent. They endorsed the establishment ideal where church and state comprised a unity, neither subor-
dinate one to the other. The *Critic* was strong in its devotion to national
institutions and firmly against the modernist political and religious inno-
vations so bloodily brought about in Revolutionary and Napoleonic
France.

The Tractarians' direct association with the *Critic* began in 1836
when Newman agreed to supply its High Church editor, James Shergold
Boone, with "four sheets [64 pages] quarterly."[20] At this time Newman
remained in general agreement with the High Churchmen over Church
affairs and thus the request for a Tractarian contribution to the *Critic*
was unremarkable. Nonetheless, the timing of the request was auspi-
cious, given Newman's (private) rejection that year of the branch idea of
the Church of England's catholicism. As we have noted earlier, this precept, held dear by a large number of High Churchmen, was now at
the mercy of someone whose allegiance to the Church of England was
weakening steadily. Quickly, Boone himself felt the wrath of Newman,
who rapidly expressed his "disappointment" and "great annoyance"
with some of Boone's editorial selections, as well as the content of his
own commentary.[21] Boone had had the temerity, in Newman's view, to
write an article on Dr. R. D. Hampden, Oxford's Regius Professor of
Divinity and a man the Tractarians despised for his theological liberalism. In so doing, Boone had committed the sin of mere evenhandedness
and thereby had shown himself deficient in judgment. Newman rejected
Boone's explanations and began complaining to Joshua Watson about
his fitness as editor. Newman stepped up his campaign to oust Boone in
1837 by informing Watson that he would be "unable to send any additional contributions" to the magazine.[22] By this time Boone had realized
that his editorship had been undermined irretrievably, and so he chose
to resign rather than involve himself in an all-out struggle with Newman
for control of the *Critic*. In November 1837, a relieved Watson wrote to
Newman to say that Boone had submitted his resignation, as well as to
seek an assurance that "the usual supplies will not be cut off from the
next number."[23] Newman gave him a positive reply, and the *Critic* was
back on its normal course.

Or was it? Newman had given this hitherto High Church organ a stiff editorial jolt. With Boone's resignation he now saw his way clear to push the *Critic* in the more radical direction he wished it to go. In July 1838, he became editor, and the magazine had a new spiritual proprietor: the Oxford Movement. The well-disposed Joshua Watson had not yet begun to worry seriously about what Newman's coup might ultimately mean for the *Critic*. The apparent unity of High Churchmen and Tractarians seemed intact.

In the two years prior to Newman's assumption of editorial control of the *Critic* in 1838 various Tractarians and fellow travelers had contributed twenty-nine articles to the magazine.[24] As Newman's struggle with Boone demonstrates, he was determined to make the *Critic* "a new platform for his views."[25] This stance meant, as Beverly Tinsley observes, that "under his guidance every issue was decided in light of its coincidence with the view of the Church of Antiquity."[26]

As we have suggested, Newman's insistence that the contemporary Church must be measured strictly against its ancient begetter was highly problematic for the old High Churchmen. His increasing fondness for an interpretation of catholicism that found much to admire in the Roman system exacerbated the cleavage between the Tractarians and the "Zs." The crux of the divergence between the two parties lay in what Peter Nockles terms "patristic fundamentalism."[27] The heart of the Church of antiquity was the church fathers themselves, whose foundation and early elaboration of the Church were *sine qua non* for Newman. To the extent that England's contemporary ecclesiastical structure failed to reflect its patristic source meant that it was in error. Newman's polemic against the Church of England thus ran directly into an equally determined defense of it by High Churchmen, who rejected his impassioned antiquarianism in favor of their own view of a Church whose prerogatives remained unimpaired by its constitutional unity with the state.

As Newman continued in his editorship of the *Critic*, High Church opposition intensified. From 1838, the articles he published in the magazine were ordered in such a way as to bolster the case for the patristic interpretation of the origins of the Church of England. For almost three years, until April 1841, this meant that the establishment was attacked by the Tractarians for having become irretrievably compromised. In articles such as "Church and King," by Thomas Mozley, "Ecclesiastical Discipline," by George Bowyer, and "State of Religious Parties," by Newman himself, the supposed unity of church and state was mocked.[28] As Bowyer remarked disparagingly, the Church of England was nothing more than "a law Church,"[29] an appellation abhorrent to the Tractarian conception of the Church, but an accurate description in their eyes of the Erastian bog into which the Church had sunk under the uncaring gaze of its putative defenders at Westminster.

The Tractarian attack on the alliance of church and state continued unabated until Newman resigned from the *Critic* in the spring of 1841, whereupon it declined markedly. By this time, Newman was exhausted both physically and mentally. But more important, he was beginning to feel the unrelenting wrath of those he had criticized in the pages of the *Critic,* as well as elsewhere. The old High Churchmen were now in a constant state of alarm over what Newman or one of his colleagues might do or say next. The younger generation of Tractarians, men such as Thomas Mozley and Frederick Oakeley, wanted to make the old High Churchmen even more uncomfortable than they already were and were calling upon Newman to become even more transparent in his endorsement of (Roman) Catholicism. The pressure of this situation became too great for Newman, and so he resigned, leaving the *Critic* in the hands of Mozley who would soon alienate the magazine's old constituency completely and thereby bring its publication to an end. Given what the *Critic* had become in the hands of the Tractarians, most High Churchmen could not have been happier. "The relief at the termination of this unceasing sore," rejoiced the High Churchman William Palmer of Worcester College, "was indescribable."[30] The same cannot be said of Joshua Watson, however. He had suffered Newman patiently, believing in the necessity of at least part of the Tractarians' catholic renewal campaign, and had refused to break with him. "We must not desert the Oxford men,"[31] Watson's friend, eventual biographer, and fellow High Churchman Edward Churton wrote to him in 1843. And Watson did not desert Newman, leaving any desertion to his erstwhile friend to carry out two years later.

The departure of Newman from the *British Critic* is one of the events that spelled out clearly the divergent paths of the extremist Tractarians and the old High Churchmen. Newman's quest was to find an answer to his own question, "Where is the Church?"[32] It was not enough to present the Church of antiquity as the model; the need for a contemporary manifestation of it must be acknowledged and then fulfilled. Ultimately of course, in 1845, Newman gave up on Anglicanism. He could not find an acceptable Church in England and thus made public his declaration that he had found the true Church in Rome.

Newman's break with the Church of England and with his long-standing Anglican colleagues and friends forced a reconstitution of the Oxford Movement and a reordering of the relationship between those Tractarians who had rejected Newman's stance and remained loyal to the Church of England and the old High Churchmen. For Keble and Pusey, the years immediately following 1845 saw them accept the universalist idea of the Church to the exclusion of the branch theory. But their view of universalism differed sharply from Newman's, who now, if not before, saw Rome ever and always as the embodiment of the church catholic. For Keble and Pusey, the church catholic was found not in Rome, but rather in the ancient, undivided church. The Church of England, therefore, was in waiting for the judgment of an ecumenical council. Rome, as a consequence, was not the sole arbiter of catholicity, as Newman would have it, but suffered from the same mark of schism as did the Church of England. "We stand as orthodox Catholics upon a constant virtual appeal to the Ecumenical voice of the church," stated Keble defiantly[33]

What then of the old High Churchmen in the mid-to-late 1840s? They were both relieved and saddened by Newman's departure for Rome. They reacted to Newman's succession and responded to the continued presence in the Church of Tractarian loyalists by reasserting the old tradition. William Palmer argued that the English Church was every bit as catholic as the Roman. Indeed, Rome was schismatical, not Canterbury, because it was the former who had separated from the Eastern Churches, as well as from the English. "The mere fact of not being in communion with Rome was no proof of schism," declared Palmer.[34] Despite confident statements of this kind, post-1845 High Churchmen continued to exist in a delicate position, a kind of *via media* of their own construction. Not "too decidedly Catholic" or "too decidedly Anglican" was the description given to the High Church balancing act by one of its most notable practitioners, Charles Wordsworth, bishop of St. Andrews. The wounds were deep, and it was not until around 1860 that High Churchmen regrouped sufficiently in order to more clearly enunciate their position, doing so in part through a commitment to missionary Anglicanism and the establishment of the Church overseas.[35] More importantly, however, the 1860s marked the beginning of a development that would have a profound effect on the continuing relations between High Churchmen and Tractarians: ritualism.

In the early days of the Oxford Movement ritualism or elaborate ceremonial within the Anglican liturgy seems not to have been of vital concern to the Tractarians. Even though their project of Church renewal entailed restoring some ritualistic practices lost to the English Reformation—such as making the sign of the Cross—the Tractarians' most important concerns during the 1830s lay, as we have seen, elsewhere. Recently, however, the scholarship of Nigel Yates and Mats Selen has begun to alter this traditional picture.[36] They suggest persuasively that the original Tractarians' clear interest in ritual made it possible for their successors to so readily incorporate the externals of Roman Catholic practice into the Anglican service. As we shall see in Chapter 4, the Gothic revival embodied the physical manifestation of this drive to catholicize the Church of England. Gothic churches came to symbolize the difference between sacramental worship and lower forms of Christian congregationalism. The Ecclesiological Society influenced churches in their adoption of ceremonial and in their cultivation of a sense of spiritual mystery. Awe and devotion became the desired emotions engendered by Anglo-Catholic worship.

For the old High Churchmen, the rise of ritualism was unwelcome. It meant the continuation of the rift between them and the heirs of the Tractarians. Pusey, much to dismay of the "Zs," seemed to offer too much by way of leadership to the ritualists, even though as we suggest in Chapter 4 he was loath to consider himself leader of any party, least of all theirs. He clashed regularly over ritualism with notable High Churchmen, such as his own diocesan, Samuel Wilberforce, and Walter Hook, who believed himself to be under siege by Pusey-inspired "papist" hordes at St. Saviour's, Leeds. As for Pusey and Palmer, they never reconciled fully, and near the end of Palmer's life, he lamented "that Pusey's proceedings as the self-constituted leader of the Tractarian party often caused me very great unhappiness."[37]

Naturally, Palmer was ridiculed by the Anglo-Catholics in much the same way that he and the other old High Churchmen had been accused of clinging to an outmoded position on the Church by Newman and Froude a generation and more before. In the Gorham controversy in the 1850s, and then later in the spirited debate over the Public Worship Regulation Act in the 1870s, Pusey stood apart from High Churchmen, whose sympathies he had lost almost completely. The pattern of disaffection between the Tractarian and High Church parties established during the 1830s remained in place long after the original heat and light had gone out of the Oxford Movement. The memories of churchmen are especially long, it would seem.

A key churchman in the move by many from the older Tractarian position to Anglo-Catholic ritualism was Alexander Heriot Mackonochie (1825–87), whose most important years were spent as rector of St. Alban's, Holborn, in London.[38] Mackonochie went up to Oxford in 1845, and there came slowly under the influence of Tractarianism as it emerged from its Newman period. Upon taking his degree, Mackonochie embarked on a series of clerical appointments which took him through the 1850s. In 1862, he arrived at the recently constructed St. Alban's, designed by the doyen of neo-Gothic architects, William Butterfield.

Under Mackonochie's direction St. Alban's established itself as the leading ritualist church in London by the end of the 1860s. In heightening ceremonial Mackonochie brought on considerable ridicule by Protestant defenders of the Church of England, as represented by the Church Association. In 1867, the attacks on Mackonochie and St. Alban's took the form of a lawsuit, the harbinger of a litigious decade to come. Pusey supported Mackonochie because the ritualism of St. Alban's was endorsed by the congregation, a requirement for its introduction anywhere, Pusey believed.[39]

While ritualism was never to the taste of most Anglicans, its expansion does suggest the Oxford Movement's varied impact on their religious practices. Indeed, as Owen Chadwick declares: "The Oxford

Movement was of decisive importance to the religion of the English."[40] Decisive because in the long journey through its High Church forebears and its formulation in the hearts and hands of Newman, Keble, Froude, Pusey, and others, it deepened the way in which religious practice was conceived and carried out within the Church of England. Of course, this transformation occurred in the midst of strife. As has been examined above, as well as later in this study, opposition to the Tractarian project was often sharp and usually long, but it was not, ultimately, debilitating.

In large part the religious success of the Oxford Movement must be attributed to John Keble. Pastoral duties dominated his thinking. Even though Keble had been a brilliant undergraduate, moral worth far outstripped intellectual prowess in his personal hierarchy of values. Keble's religiosity was of utmost importance in facilitating the dissemination of the moral ideal of the Oxford Movement, especially to country parishes. The religion of the Tractarian rural parish is epitomized by John's brother Thomas Keble, as well as by Isaac Williams and George Prevost, the "Bisley Tractarians," so named because of Williams's incumbency of Bisley parish.[41] Away from the noise and controversy of Oxford these men and others like them sought to live and preach the Tractarian message of liturgical worship, eucharistic communion, and intercessory prayer. In his "National Apostasy" sermon of 1833 John Keble had lamented the "neglecting or undervaluing [of] ordinary duties, more especially those of a devotional kind" by those in positions of ecclesiastical and civil authority.[42] In the face of the "fashionable liberality of this generation," Keble counseled "intercession" and "remonstrance" to return England to the right Christian path.[43] In the example of the men of Bisley the life of quiet devotion, the Kebleian Tractarian ideal, was lived out.

Keble himself, as we know, was the best example of his own prescription for religious devotion. His deep belief in sacramental religion manifested itself in frequent celebrations of the Eucharist at Hursley, where he spent most of his Anglican pastoral life. Of course, *The Christian Year* (1827), a minor work of poetry but a major work of Anglican devotionalism, made him well known in his time, but its popularity had no perceptible effect on his retiring character. In the 1820s, Newman had needed to penetrate Keble's wall of reserve in order to be introduced to the religious power of the catholic tradition in the Church of England. For Newman, this introduction proved a revelation, while for Keble the Church had ever been thus.

It was at Hursley where Keble put into practice the religious precepts of the Oxford Movement. In addition to increasing the number of eucharistic celebrations there he stressed the importance of church-going as a "service" to God rather than as a means for individual edification. Daily matins and evensong were introduced. Holiness was Keble's byword; and as his most important biographer, Georgina Battiscombe, observes, "it was his destiny to be an inspiration."[44] His moral idealism included having no social interaction with those he considered enemies of the Church, and this meant anyone "even faintly tinged with Liberalism."[45] Occasionally this stance made parish life difficult for Keble but he clung to his conception of right and wrong on this point, and it shaped his later belief that the "complete secularization of men's minds" was perilous for all religion.[46]

The specter of religious "liberalism"—meaning the decline of dogma—haunted all the Tractarians. Keble chose to oppose its spread through the counterexample of a life of personal holiness and devotion. Newman, on the other hand, preferred intellectual combat on behalf of the (catholic) religious principle. By the early 1840s, Newman was relentless in blaming the Protestant Reformers for introducing into the Church the questioning spirit, the outcome of which could only be deleterious—if not debilitating—to the religious principle. As Newman wrote to a friend in 1841: "The spirit of lawlessness came in at the Reformation—and Liberalism is its offspring."[47] Dogma was intrinsic to religion, Newman argued with increasing ferocity. A religion without doctrine is a contradiction, an "unreal" state, he believed.[48] But the Protestant dependence on Scripture as the fount of doctrine was mistaken, Newman argued, because of the haphazard nature of biblical writings and the presence of implicit doctrines "in places expected and unexpected." Though inspired, the Bible was not designed, as liberal Protestantism insisted. The result of this insistence is to ask of Scripture an impossibility. "The true system of religion"[49] cannot be deduced from a faith centered in Scripture, Newman maintained. But as long as Protestants continued to demand such from the Bible they would continue to be bedeviled by the existence of a plethora of sects each espousing its own so-called authentic view. Regrettably and ironically, he argued, the only unity that exists in the Protestant religious world is its uniform opposition to the claim that the church universal is the locus of Christian authority.

Newman's attack on Protestantism as the Trojan horse of liberal-ism formed the heart of his antimodern polemic during his Anglican period. His Roman Catholic years saw an expansion of this theme to include a general defense of religion, which came to characterize his stance as the most important Christian apologist of the nineteenth cen-tury. This feature of Newman's thinking, however, is outside the scope of the present study.

The third member of the Tractarian triumvirate, Pusey, used his considerable scholarly weight, his social position, and his authority within the University of Oxford to impress upon Anglicans the indis-pensability of proper forms of worship and the necessity for these to embody a mystical reverence for God and the Church. In 1840, by which time the Oxford Movement was commonly called Puseyism, Pusey set out six features encapsulating his putative namesake's meaning:

1. High thoughts of the two sacraments.
2. High estimate of Episcopacy as God's ordinance.
3. High estimate of the visible Church as the Body wherein we are made and continue to be members of Christ.
4. Regard for ordinances, as directing our devotions and disciplining us, such as daily public prayers, fasts and feasts, etc.
5. Regard for the visible part of devotion, such as the decoration of the house of God, which acts insensibly on the mind.
6. Reverence for and deference to the ancient Church, of which our own Church is looked upon as the representative to us, and by whose views and doctrines we interpret our own Church when her meaning is questioned or doubtful; in a word, reference to the ancient Church, instead of the Reformers, as the ultimate expounder of meaning of our Church.[50]

For Pusey, the Oxford Movement's chief purpose was to deepen the Anglican religion, recalling its ancient forms and recasting its mystical features. He was its *doctor mysticus,* as the first Swedish historian of the Movement, Yngve Brilioth, called him.[51] As the discussion of Tractarian theology later in this chapter suggests, Pusey was concerned primarily with the individual soul's union with God, the divine indwelling of the human heart. This idea, in Owen Chadwick's view, more than any other, marks Pusey's unique contribution to the theology of the Oxford Movement.[52] In its translation to religious practice came Pusey's commitment to communitarian forms of worship and the centrality of the Eucharist to both communion with God and fellowship with humankind.[53]

Whether in Keble's rural pastoralism, Newman's relentless intellectualism, or Pusey's mystical devotionalism, the Tractarians owed much to their High Church forebears, for it was from them that they derived their central preoccupation with the authority of the Church and their apprehension of the spiritual and liturgical content of correct worship and devoted service.

Peter Nockles does a masterful job of recounting the ways and means by which high churchmanship brought its orthopraxy to bear on the Tractarians.[54] Denial of self was a controlling aspiration of the Oxford men. Froude, as we shall see in Chapter 3, was especially committed to the ascetic life. But in a way that left considerably less room for caricature and ridicule, Newman, Keble, and Pusey also attempted to deepen their spirituality through self-mortification. The inspiration that they may have drawn from St. Paul's peripatetic progress in the wilderness where he was sustained by a diet of locusts and wild honey is unclear; that drawn from High Church spirituality is more evident. A number of seventeenth- and eighteenth-century High Church writers extolled the virtues of asceticism, including the immensely influential William Law, author of *A Serious Call to a Devout and Holy Life* (1729), which became a kind of High Church catechism. Law endorsed fasting and celibacy, and this strain of High Church thinking on the acceptability of extreme forms of spirituality found ready acceptance by Froude, as his private journals, published as the *Remains,* show clearly. Pusey too was very receptive to asceticism, making it a central feature of his home and family life and writing about its virtues in numbers 18 and 66 of the *Tracts for the Times,* where he points to fasting as "a Christian duty," arguing that "wherever there is regularity, there must be forms; . . . every Christian feeling must have its appropriate vehicle of expression."[55]

Many High Churchmen, however, rejected the position held by Law and the Tractarians. This other strain of thought, called by contemporaries Warburtonian after William Warburton, the Georgian-era bishop of Gloucester and Anglican divine, and Tillotsonian after John Tillotson, archbishop of Canterbury in the seventeenth century, disparaged the "enthusiasm" of devotional asceticism. They thought such asceticism extreme and ultimately designed to draw attention away from God to the ascetic himself. The Tractarians, however, were deeply attracted to Law's ascetic ideal and made it part of their ethos. The divergence in view between the Tractarians and some of the old High Churchmen—notably, Godfrey Faussett, Oxford's Lady Margaret Professor of Divinity—deepened the rift between them, especially when combined with other features of their disagreement. But the most important of the High Churchmen, Joshua Watson, did not censure the Tractarians for their championing of the ascetic ideal.[56] As in most other areas of his contact with the Oxford men Watson was very tolerant, always believing that their contribution to the Church of England outweighed whatever internecine strife they engendered.

For the Tractarians, the ascetic ideal alone could not embody their desire for a religion of feeling. The evangelicals may have made "vital" religion their own distinguishing mark, but the Tractarians too yearned for a religion of greater emotional resonance than that practiced by the "high and dry" orthodox High Churchmen. Emotional coldness and personal reticence marked this style of churchmanship, in the view of the Tractarians, and they sought to recast their own churchmanship in a mold of romantic spirituality.

The romantic inheritance of the Tractarians is well known, especially that bequeathed by the poets William Wordsworth and Robert Southey. In the *Christian Year* Keble made overt this inheritance and among his coreligionists reinforced the idea that their religious practice need not emulate the remote and frigid ways of many of the old High Churchmen. Keble's poetry provided an avenue of restrained emotional freedom along which the Tractarians could travel in an attempt to establish their own rubric of spirituality.[57] This may be seen, for example, in

Keble's *Christian Year* poem "Morning," later part of the hymn "New Every Morning Is the Love": "The trivial round, the common task, would furnish all we ought to ask; room to deny ourselves; a road to bring us, daily, nearer God."[58] As Nockles observes rightly: "The revived High Church spirituality of Keble's *Christian Year* exemplified a restraint and self-effacement that was in constructive tension with the warmth and feeling it also embodied."[59] This tension revealed itself in the Tractarians' commitment to reserve in both devotional temper and, more important, in "the communicating of religious knowledge," as Isaac Williams would detail in his tract published in 1837.[60] Williams argued that in God's dealings with his human creation there was "a very remarkable holding back of sacred and important truths."[61] This "economy" in revelation was an ancient idea that Newman had long been probing and which had been an important feature of his *Arians of the Fourth Century* (1833). In the same vein Williams was sure that the communication of certain religious ideas "was injurious to persons unworthy of them,"[62] and the articulation of this belief set off a firestorm of controversy, especially among evangelicals, who denounced this restriction on the Gospel and its full apprehension by all.[63]

In this area of the Tractarians' religious project, however, there was an essential commonality of view with the old High Churchmen. Some among them, such as Henry Norris of the *British Critic* and William Copeland, believed strongly in reserve, and Norris in particular had condemned the Bible Society (also denounced by Newman) for its indiscriminate distribution of Scripture to the illiterate and unlearned, who were unequipped to understand it without proper guidance. There was a definite aversion to this practice, which those who espoused reserve considered a "casting of pearls before swine." Scripture, Norris wrote to a friend, is not "the instrument of conversion—but the repository of divine knowledge for the perfecting of those already converted. I mean that it is the children's bread and not to be cast to dogs."[64]

Reserve in communicating religious knowledge was a principle that fit smoothly with the Tractarians' well-developed belief in the mysterious nature of religion. As we know, Pusey was especially receptive to mysticism, and in part he was responding to a High Church imperative when arguing for the continuation and the deepening of sacramental symbolism. The writings of Richard Hooker and Bishop Joseph Butler of Durham were vital to this spiritual inheritance. Newman, too, thought highly of Butler in this regard, remarking that his "wonderfully gifted intellect caught the idea which had actually been the rule of the Primitive Church, of teaching the more sacred truths by rites and ceremonies."[65]

It is suggested, then, that the importance attached to ceremonial and ritual by the Tractarians emerged from a High Church tradition which demanded reverence and reserve as necessary to proper worship. The critical spirit of the age—so well represented by the Noetics, for example—was utterly contemptible to the Tractarians, whose spirituality could never allow for that same kind of intellectual, Protestant confrontationalism to characterize their religious practice. Newman's dramatic habit of falling to his knees before the St. Mary's Church altar in Oxford was a manifestation of this belief in spiritual surrender and when imitated by undergraduates came to offer a physical signature of the Movement's demanding, or as some would criticize, its insidious, religiosity.[66]

As elaborated in Chapter 4, the Gothic architectural revival physically embodied the Tractarian spiritual ideal. But for the Tractarians, spiritual excellence of course was of much greater importance than its external analogue. The proper liturgy was the means by which such excellence could be advanced. Here, as in so many other areas, the Tractarians owed much to the High Churchmen, especially those whose influence helped produce the 1662 version of the Book of Common Prayer. This repository of the Anglican liturgy came under attack periodically by latitudinarian revisionists in the early years of the nineteenth century. The Tractarians defended the Prayer Book together with High Churchmen against such attacks even though they were ready to push for their own revisions based on a restoration of those doctrines purged from the Anglican liturgy by the Protestant Reformers. Newman, especially, was exercised on this point and at great length in the *Tracts* argued that the Prayer Book could be explained and defended by examining the Roman Breviary in which "there is so much of excellence and beauty. . . . Whatever is good and true in those Devotions will be claimed, and on reasonable grounds, for the Church Catholic in opposition to the Roman Church."[67]

While Newman was yet still within the Anglican fold, his endorsement of the Breviary was unwelcome to High Churchmen, who thought it a dangerous tack to take in order to spur revision and likely to result in increased feelings of Anglican liturgical imperfection which could not be assuaged.[68] Froude, too, was critical of the Prayer Book and in *Tract* no. 63 had argued for the acceptance by the Church of the Prayer Book's derivation from "remote antiquity" and the need for the restoration of its ancient forms.[69] The common features of the world's main liturgical forms "resemble one another too much to have grown up independently," and the closer the Prayer Book could be brought to the Roman Breviary in particular, the more authentic it would be.[70]

Debates over the Anglican liturgy would continue and become especially heated in the late 1840s. The Tractarians' direct interest waned after 1841, however, and for Newman ceased altogether by 1843. Later Anglo-Catholics did not take up the banner of reform mostly in an attempt to heal the rift between themselves and the High Churchmen, which had been exposed fully by Newman's secession.

But if the public campaign for liturgical revision declined, the strong desire for personal holiness in Tractarian religious practice yielded a consistent interest in manuals for private devotion. For radical Tractarians such as W. G. Ward, Frederick Oakeley, and Frederick Faber, the Roman Breviary became the devotional source of choice and to which Anglican devotional practice was unfavorably compared. Pusey's response to the relentless catholicizing of this aspect of the Movement by his younger colleagues was to "adapt" Roman Catholic devotional books, such as Surin's *Foundations of the Spiritual Life,* for Anglican usage.[71] But in so doing he satisfied no one; the young lions of the Movement were preternaturally opposed to what they took to be desperate measures by Pusey to staunch the bleeding of dissatisfied Anglicans to Rome, and High Churchmen thought the exercise to be yet another mistaken concession by the Movement gone awry. As Bishop Phillpotts lamented, "All but divine honour is ascribed to the Virgin Mary" in the books Pusey chose to adapt.[72]

The Tractarians' ability to inspire both extreme disaffection and extreme devotion made for a deep impact on the religion of the Victorian Church of England and on the Christian landscape of England generally.[73] Such was their main achievement; some would say it was their only achievement. But leave it to Owen Chadwick to be nearest the mark in his summation of the religious influence of the Oxford Tractarians: "They succeeded, far beyond the expectations of many, in transforming the atmosphere of English worship, in deepening the content of English prayer, in lifting English eyes, not only to their own insular tradition, but to the treasures of the Catholic centuries, whether ancient or modern."[74] If such was the true character of the tendency to Romanism William Palmer of Worcester College had accused the Tractarians of displaying, then for them and their mid-nineteenth-century heirs it was a charge borne gladly.[75]

The theology of the Tractarians, as the foundation of their religion, is a topic of perennial interest to those intent on seeking a fundamental understanding of the Oxford Movement. Among the Tractarians, Newman's fertile intellect produced an immense amount of theological writing, and his is the most important, though not the only, voice in this regard. Much of Newman's theology was presented in public from the pulpit of St. Mary's, the university church in Oxford, where he was vicar from 1828 to 1843. Newman's sermons formed the cornerstone of his pastoral ministry, as well as being one of the most prominent platforms for the airing of the themes and ideas of the Movement.[76] To a lesser extent, Pusey and Keble (notwithstanding the latter's famous Assize sermon accorded such prominence in the history of the Movement by Newman in the *Apologia*) used their pulpits also to expound a theology which bore the Tractarian hallmarks of sacramentalism, baptismal regeneration, patristic foundations, and the apostolic succession.

In this part of the chapter we will explore the theology of the Oxford Movement by examining closely the words contained in some of the important Tractarian publications, especially Newman's *Parochial and Plain Sermons* and the *Tracts for the Times*. Some of Pusey's sermons, also, are of value in more fully apprehending Tractarian theology. In elaborating a theology, the Tractarians charted their own course through a melange of High Churchmen, evangelicals, latitudinarians, and Roman Catholics. Tractarian theology and the context in which it was articulated were shaped in important ways by these competing traditions, and this multifaceted and vital influence on the Tractarians needs to be understood in order to see Tractarian theology for what it was in the 1830s and 1840s.

The Tractarians did not see themselves as the progenitors of a new theology. Indeed, for Keble especially, innovation in theology as in most everything else in religion and in life was to be avoided. Rather, Keble and the other leaders of the Oxford Movement saw themselves as reasserting the Church of England's catholic heritage, which in their view, had fallen into abject disuse at the hands of an establishment gone apostate. To recover this lost catholic "ethos" the Tractarians understood it to be their task to revive the catholic tradition of the English Church by harking back, in the first place, to the teachings of the Fathers of the ancient church. Newman's interest in the early church was sparked by his influential Oriel colleague Richard Whateley in the mid-1820s. In 1828, as Newman recounts in the *Apologia,* he plunged into a thorough reading of the works of the Fathers.[77] Then, two years later in 1830, Rivington, the publisher, invited Newman to contribute a volume on the Council of Nicaea to their Theological Library, and this project allowed him to conduct an intensive study of the early church.

Newman's investigation of the Council meant a close study of the history of the Arian heresy of the fourth century, with which it had dealt. Newman's historical and literary encounter with Arius, who had been a priest from the outskirts of Alexandria, was decisive in shaping his devotion to the Fathers and in creating his reliance on the early church as the foundation of all Christian theology and Church practice.

As Newman understood it, the controversy emerged early in the fourth century when Arius contended that Christ the Son was not coequal with God but merely his creature: "There was a time when the Son was not."[78] This position was in defiance of earlier teaching, especially that of Origen, that the Father and the Son were "of one substance." In 325, a synod of bishops met at Nicaea in Asia Minor to rule on a number of matters, the most important of which was the "heresy" being taught by this troublesomely unorthodox Egyptian. The bishops ruled Arius to be in "error" and wrote "identical in being" into their confession of faith to describe the Godhead. For a number of years the "Arian heresy" continued to percolate in the Church until it was condemned irrevocably at the Council of Constantinople in 381. It was in this manner that many theological crises in the ancient Church were dealt with, and it was also in this way that the Church consolidated its power and authority, moving the building blocks of Catholic civilization into place.

For Newman, the study of this event in the Church's early history was revolutionary. In the book that resulted from his research, *The Arians of the Fourth Century* (1833), Newman set out the issue at hand, the error propagated by Arius, and the means by which this error was revealed and defeated. In so doing he confirmed in his own mind the necessity of creeds and the need for the Church to develop doctrine. The "dogmatic principle" was burned into Newman's intellect through the challenge accorded the Church by Arius. The Church's champion at the time, and the chief foe of Arianism all his life, was Athanasius (c. 296–373). A deacon in service to his bishop at Nicaea, Athanasius fought for years for the doctrine of consubstantiality but did not live to see it adopted by the Church. But with the Nicene orthodoxy's eventual adoption at Constantinople in 381 Athanasius's faith was rewarded. In *Arians,* Athanasius is Newman's great hero. "After a life of contest," Newman writes admiringly, "prolonged, in spite of the hardships he encountered, beyond the age of seventy years, he fell asleep in peaceable possession of the Churches for which he had suffered."[79] Athanasius's relentless devotion to truth and dogma became the standard by which Newman judged the church fathers in general. He came to use the same standard to judge contemporary churchmen as well.

For Newman, as for the other Oxford men, Athanasius's theology—patristic theology generally—was practical, and not speculative, in that it was directed at the essential truth of Christianity: Christ himself.[80] Patristic theology was also experiential, although not in an atomistic, individualist sense, but rather in a different and fuller understanding of "personhood" based on the personhood manifested in the Trinity. As Nicholas Lossky remarks: "For in this perspective, a 'person' is by definition a being-in-communion, a relational being who cannot be saved by himself alone."[81] Here is where the indispensability of the communitarian Church came into Tractarian thinking. The fount of the Christian community is the Church, they believed, the place where persons in communion with God can come into communion with their fellow creatures.

Newman's first foray into the history and theology of the Fathers revealed to him also the principle of economy used in the early church by which certain dogmas were kept hidden or shadowed awaiting a fuller explication once the Church had achieved a greater maturity. This principle was applicable also to the individual believer, Newman believed, whose faith would be best nurtured by the slow revelation of dogma. Newman argued that the withholding of theological truth from Christian believers might be necessary, since the Church's "mysteries are but the expressions in human language of truths to which the human mind is unequal."[82] But to ward off the inevitable criticism from the evangelicals that such a principle of economy is secretive and reserved, Newman was careful to enjoin the maintenance of "substantial truth in our use of the economical method."[83] Newman's point was that the holiness of the essentials of the Christian religion must be respected and should not be subjected to the kind of less than reverent approach employed by evangelicals, for example, in order to evoke an emotional response from hearers of the Gospel. The true believer must respond not emotionally but with awe and humble adoration. Instead, "now," scolded Newman, "we allow ourselves publicly to canvass the most solemn truths in a careless or fiercely argumentative way; truths, which it is as useless as it is unseemly to discuss in public, as being attainable only by the sober and watchful, by slow degrees, with dependence on the Giver of wisdom, and with strict obedience to the light which has already been granted."[84]

Newman's words, unsurprisingly, elicited fierce objections from some Oxford churchmen. As well, his insistence that the origins of the Arian Heresy were traceable to Antioch instead of Alexandria, the traditionally accepted origin, a view which altered the genesis of the crisis, were seen as historically inaccurate. Moreover, his deep investigation into Arius left little room within the book for the Council of Nicaea itself, the publisher Rivington's expectation and the thing about which buyers of the Library expected to read. As Newman himself remarked later, his treatment of the Council "occupied at most twenty pages."[85] In the assigned task, therefore, Newman had failed. But that, it seems, mattered little to him. As a Tractarian polemic, on the other hand, *Arians* served a vitally important purpose. While Newman considered the book "inexact in thought and incorrect in language," with some "good points in it, and in some parts originality,"[86] these reservations aside, it struck Newman and the Tractarians like a thunderbolt. For Tractarian theology and for Newman himself, *Arians* made clear a reliance on antiquity and a belief in the foundations of Christianity, in "the mystical or sacramental principle."[87]

As for the other leading Tractarians, Pusey's knowledge of the church fathers likewise became deep, especially his familiarity with St. Augustine. For Pusey, the Fathers had spawned a theology that linked revelation, theological reflection, and personal experience. This unity was highly appealing to Pusey and to the other Tractarian leaders. As we shall see in Chapter 4, Pusey's spirituality was centered on the Eucharist. Patristics, on the other hand, became for him a kind of repository of the Law, rather than a spiritual guide. As Gabriel O'Donnell notes correctly, Pusey's "chief use of the Fathers was as a source of theological orthodoxy."[88]

Keble's interest in patristics centered on Irenaeus, bishop of Lyons in the second century. Irenaeus wrote of the essential unity of the two Testaments in refutation of the Gnostics and others, whose positions, while in error, were close to orthodox Christianity and thereby offered a temptation to orthodox congregations, as had been the case with Marcion and the Gnosticizing Platonist Valentine. The New Testament, according to Irenaeus, completed the moral education begun by the Old, that the two comprised a progressive revelation that declared the unfolding of the divine plan. Accordingly, Irenaeus's interpretation of the Christian faith is decidedly biblical, dependent upon the authority contained in the apostolic Bible. Given Keble's innately submissive nature it is easy to see why Irenaeus would appeal greatly to him. The accepted traditions of the early church and the Bible were paramount for Irenaeus, and he was deeply suspicious of anyone claiming a fresh revelation or radical departure from such traditions. Keble, as we know, abhorred innovation and indeed delighted in tradition for its own sake. Readily, then, Irenaeus became his patristic hero.

It is no slight to either Pusey or Keble, but merely a reflection of

the historical record, to concentrate our examination of Tractarian patristic theology on Newman. "No Anglican," states Sheridan Gilley with
probable accuracy, "has ever studied [the Fathers] with the passion and
intensity of Newman."[89] He was the chief theologian among the Tractarians, although it was Pusey who decided to expand their encounter
with the early church by formulating the idea for the *Library of the
Fathers* in 1836. Newman, however, had been thinking along the same
lines as his friend: "I fancied," he recalled in the *Apologia,* "that there
could be no rashness in giving to the world in fullest measure the teachings and the writings of the Fathers. I thought that the Church of England was substantially founded upon them."[90] Once undertaken in 1838
this massive project would last until 1885 and result in the publication of
nearly fifty volumes. The work of translation and revision was immense,
but its achievement was vital to the renewal of the catholic ideal in the
Church of England.

Newman edited a number of the volumes himself; the only year
in which no volume was produced in the long publishing run of the
Library was 1846, the year following Newman's departure for Rome.
Patristics was the theological core of the Oxford Movement, and it animated and guided Newman in his work as an Anglican cleric. One of
the most important areas in which this patristic influence can be seen is
in the multitude of sermons Newman preached at St. Mary's Church in
Oxford. Here, he was able to instruct his parishioners in the theology of
the early church and reaffirm its call on contemporary Anglicans.

For almost twenty years, from 1824 to 1843, Newman carried out
the regular duties of an Anglican priest at St. Mary's, as well as at St.
Clement's, which was also in the gift of Oriel College.[91] The focal point
of Newman's parish work were the sermons he preached every Sunday
afternoon at St. Mary's. It was traditional for an Anglican priest to write
out his sermons and then read them to the congregation; thus, it was an
easy step to publishing them, which Newman began to do to considerable public acceptance in 1834. Over the next nine years six volumes of
Parochial Sermons came out, as well as a seventh volume titled *Plain
Sermons.* In all, Newman wrote 604 sermons in his Anglican career, of
which approximately one-third were published.[92]

Newman divided his sermons into a number of categories, such as

"Practical" and "Biblical," and the sermons classified under these headings reveal Newman's mind as it developed and changed from the evangelicalism of his younger days to that of a fuller appreciation and understanding of the early church fathers.[93] Newman's position as a parish priest demanded that the sermons be mainly pastoral rather than polemical. But throughout the corpus Newman's clear intention is to instruct his listeners in the full and proper apprehension of the Church and of the Christian faith based on an explication of their biblical and patristic heritage. Impressing upon his parishioners a high view of the Church—its liturgical demands and its sacramental nature—became the central feature of Newman's preaching by the latter 1820s. As an example, a series of ten sermons preached during the winter of 1830 demonstrates well Newman's insistence on deepening the liturgical knowledge of his parishioners so that they might better understand the faith and the Church of which they were a part.[94]

Newman's "Course on the Liturgy" was anti-evangelical in intent. As we know, Newman moved away from evangelicalism in the 1820s. This move was epitomized by, among other things, his rejection of the evangelical-dominated Church Missionary Society (CMS), of which he had been Oxford secretary, in 1829–30.[95] The ten sermons that comprised the "Course" made a call for the revival of liturgy in parish churches against what Newman took to be its creeping eradication at the hands of the evangelicals. The course began on Sunday, January 31, 1830, not long after his resignation from the CMS, with Newman preaching on the service of the Christian priest, something which would be a recurring theme for all the Tractarians. The series ended ten weeks later on April 4. Methodically, Newman went through the uses of the liturgy, its teaching of Christian doctrine, and its forming of Christian character, and he appealed for its full acceptance in the life of every Christian believer. The Book of Common Prayer was a veritable liturgical treasure house in which, Newman assured his listeners,

> we have a system of doctrine, a practical lesson of holiness, and a permanent bond of peace, unity and concord—Yet My Brethren, how little do *we* feel its blessedness,—alas! What privileges have we, yet we do

not improve them.—Who are so favoured by Almighty God as we are, to whom are *continued* those blessings vouchsafed to the Primitive Church by the hands of the Apostles, but since scattered up and down the world and in many places lost by the rude pride and waywardness of men.[96]

To restore a full sense of the Anglican liturgy to his parishioners, to rescue them from the clutches of those—evangelicals and latitudinarians in particular—who would devalue the liturgic imperative, was Newman's appointed task in this series of sermons. The liturgy alone represented the Church's true nature handed down by the Fathers and kept alive in the Prayer Book. Without it, Newman warned the St. Mary's congregation week after week, the Church could not properly carry out its historic mission, nor could parishioners be instructed properly.

In this way did Newman seek to enlarge the minds of his parishioners in order for them to see more clearly "the relation of the Church to the world." This "rule," as Newman called it, was one he usually adhered to in composing his sermons.[97] Another "rule" of Newman's was that his sermons would not be "full of red-hot Tractarianism."[98] The best place to find that was in the *Tracts for the Times.* Patristic theology was much better probed in the polemical *Tracts,* where one could and did demand the complete intellectual engagement of the reader and where concern about the upsetting of long-held theological verities or the breaching of pastoral niceties was nonexistent.

The *Tracts,* as we know, were to be "short and sharp," piercing the flesh of a moribund clergy and rousing a complacent establishment. The early tracts concentrated especially on the Church's catholic heritage, arguing for its proper reassertion in the church-state unity. In "The Catholic Church" (no. 2), "Adherence to the Apostolical Succession the Safest Course" (no. 4), and "Bishops, Priests, and Deacons" (no. 12), this thrust is made clear. But one tract in particular stands out in this regard. "The Present Obligation of Primitive Practice" (no. 6) forwarded unreservedly the Tractarian case for the early church. Written by Newman, this tract struck hard at the Church's contemporary disregard of its ancient model and wondered why if Christ "set about to fulfil the law in its strictness, just as if He had lived in the generation next to Moses," the contemporary Church of England had strayed from the injunctions of the Apostles. It was to them, Newman commanded, "and not to the teachers and oracles of the present world, for the knowledge of our duty, as individuals and as members of the Christian Church" that the English Church must go for guidance.[99] Newman could see only indiscipline in the contemporary Church's straying from obedience to the practice of the apostolic succession. "Are we not bound," he asked, "not merely to acquiesce in, but zealously to maintain and inculcate the discipline which they established?"[100]

Newman and the other leading Tractarians pushed this theme relentlessly. For them, the apostolic succession was the bellwether of proper Church practice and without it no real Church could exist. Indeed, this was a first principle for the Tractarians, and from it flowed a number of associated convictions. The maintenance of the apostolic succession principle was highly problematic, however, and early in the life of the *Tracts* the essential difficulty was addressed by Newman (as well as by an anonymous writer; probably Keble). The difficulty lay in the Church of England maintaining the position that its ministers all received the apostolic commission, and did so without necessary reference to Rome, whereas those of Dissenting churches could not make this claim legitimately. Naturally, Dissenters disputed this arrogation of the succession to the Church, and to the Church alone.

The apostolic succession, Newman argued, does not belong to Rome alone, however. The Reformation may have spawned Dissenting Protestantism, but it did not rupture the right and the duty of the Church of England to claim the apostolic succession as its own and insist on its continued practice. In a classic defense of the "branch" theory of Anglicanism, Newman protested that "the English Church did *not* revolt from those who in that day had authority by succession of the Apostles. . . . The Church then by its rulers and officers reformed itself. There was no new Church founded among us, but the rights and the true doctrines of the Ancient existing Church were asserted and established."[101] Thus to now oppose the Church was to oppose God's ordinance and be left in the position of having to "invent" an ordinance with no basis in proper authority. Of course, for Newman and the Tractarians, Dissenters, while important, comprised the second tier of enemies; the first were the Erastians within the Church itself who had neglected the apostolic succession and thereby weakened the Anglican body.

The "quest for authority," to borrow the title of Rune Imberg's study of the *Tracts*,[102] was central to the Tractarian project, especially to Newman's own thinking. The *Tracts* became an ideal method for the working out of a theology in which authority could be appealed to and a Church model established. Newman's early tracts, written between 1833 and 1835, created for the Oxford Movement a theology grounded in the imperatives of the early church. In numbers 38 and 41, the "Via Media" tracts, both published in 1834, Newman praises the Church of England for having taken the middle way, "the VIA MEDIA between it and Popery."[103] But, in recent times, especially with the advent of the evangelical movement in the eighteenth century, the Church had erred on the side of Protestantism, Newman charged. This error had been assisted by the degenerative hand of the state. Consequently, the balance had been lost and was in urgent need of restoration. The "glory" of the English Church, its ability to chart a middle way, had to be reasserted. In order for this reassertion to take place the clergy had been exhorted by Newman in the first tract to "act up to your professions."[104] As ordained priests of the Church they had a responsibility to think honestly about where such authority comes from. "On *what* are we to rest our authority, when the state deserts us?" Newman's exhortation continues as he answers his own rhetorical question: "There are some who rest their divine mission on their . . . temporal distinctions. . . . I fear we have neglected the real ground on which our authority is built,—OUR APOSTOLICAL DESCENT." The task of bishops and clergy was to affirm this truth and be unafraid in declaring it wherever required, in pulpit and Parliament alike. "CHOOSE YOUR SIDE" in the struggle between Church and State, Newman commanded his readership.

In the "Via Media" tracts Newman is able to delineate clearly the Movement's goal of the rejuvenation of the clergy, at least in its early phase. The other features of the Tractarian ideal—namely the Church visible, sacramentalism, and catholicity—flowed from this early belief in the Church of England's essential correctness. According to the Tract-

arians, only by a consistent and clear call to the ordinances of the ancient
Church could the English Church revive itself and reverse the Erastian
tide that was threatening to wash it out to sea.

A bulwark against this kind of destruction was the episocopate.
Newman's view of bishops, particularly his own diocesan, was exalted
always. He understood bishops to be the direct representatives of Christ
and in them were found both wisdom and, more important, authority.
Indeed, "my own bishop was my Pope; I knew no other; the successor
of the Apostles, the Vicar of Christ," Newman recalled in the *Apologia.*[105] He was supremely confident in his theological position in these
early days of the Movement. And his position hinged upon three things:
his commitment to the "principle of dogma," a "definite religious teaching," and "my then view of the Church of Rome."[106] Together this
three-pronged position enabled Newman, as the most important and
most public Tractarian theologian, to attack almost fearlessly his enemies
and at the same time draw to himself and to the Movement supporters
whose ardor for the position enunciated eventually, in many cases, out-
did his own.

Keble's theological contribution to the Movement is seen most
clearly in the *Tracts*. Keble's early tracts were close in content and spirit
to Newman's. All of Keble's tracts relate to the priestly ministry in one
form or another. In "Adherence to the Apostolical Succession the Safest
Course" (no. 4), published in 1833, Keble stressed the absolute necessity
that a priest or minister have a sacred commission from Christ to carry
out his work. If not, then there is, in Keble's staccato words, "nothing,
properly, *sacred* about him."[107] Indeed, Keble maintained strongly and
in defiance of Dissenters, the Church of England and its adherence to
the Apostolic Succession meant that it was "THE ONLY CHURCH IN THIS
REALM WHICH HAS A RIGHT TO BE QUITE SURE THAT SHE HAS THE LORD'S
BODY TO GIVE TO HIS PEOPLE."[108]

Keble's most significant theological contribution to the Movement
came in 1841 with the publication of what would be the penultimate
tract in the series, number 89, "On the Mysticism Attributed to the
Early Fathers of the Church."[109] In it, Keble launched an attack on
Protestants and their penchant to devalue the writings of the Fathers,
to "demystify" in today's parlance, their theology. Keble argued that

"mysticism," as defined by certain Protestants, did not compromise moral truth, but that the Old Testament offered many examples of allegorical teaching. The Protestant demand for literalism was rejected because it severely misread the text and forced Scripture into an interpretation limited by the reader's own time-bound prejudice.

Unfortunately for the Tractarians, Keble's tract came out during a time when the Movement was under steady attack for its "papist" sympathies. Mysticism, however explained, was not something that could deflect this charge. Keble was fully aware of the probability that the tract would give offense.[110] But such was the price he was willing to pay in order to explicate more completely the Movement's "sacramental" theology.

The *Tracts* also provided Pusey with an opportunity to run his colors farther up the Tractarian mast. His public alignment with the Tractarians in January 1834 came about via a tract, number 18, on fasting.[111] Much more important theologically, however, was his series on baptism, numbers 67, 68, and 69, which came out the following year. In these tracts Pusey took aim at the Protestant Reformers, especially Huldrych Zwingli, whom he blamed for deceiving Christians and forcing upon them the idea that baptismal regeneration was unscriptural. On the contrary, Pusey argued, baptismal regeneration "was, for fourteen centuries, the doctrine of the universal Church of GOD."[112] In Scripture baptism was connected always with regeneration, Pusey maintained. Zwingli, however, had corrupted this historical position and did so with "a character and frame of mind decidedly rationalistic: he was comparatively little of a theologian, and but ill acquainted in detail with the character and teaching of the early Church: he had not been educated as a theologian, nor was his mind well trained."[113]

Pusey's baptismal tracts naturally caused a great stir among evangelicals. The evangelical *Christian Observer* took the position that Pusey's theology made him fit only to teach at the Catholic college of Maynooth in Ireland or, better yet, at the Vatican.[114] The Tractarians, on the other hand, could not have been more pleased with Pusey's strong presence in the pages of the *Tracts*. Pusey's high position at Oxford as Regius Professor of Hebrew made the Tractarians a group to be reckoned with, and Pusey's "influence was felt at once," recalled Newman in the *Apologia*.

"He saw that there ought to be more sobriety, more gravity, more careful pains, more sense of responsibility in the Tracts and in the whole Movement. It was through him that the character of the Tracts was changed."[115] High praise, indeed. The Tractarians recognized Pusey's deep theological learning and were eager to have it at their disposal, especially after the rousing nature of the initial tracts.

Baptismal regeneration was a kind of litmus test for Tractarian theology, and the advocacy of it by the Tractarians was a source of much controversy during the main years of the Movement and later, as we shall see in Chapter 4. Newman had begun to struggle with this thorny theological issue in the mid-1820s. Evangelicals believed that spiritual regeneration came with conversion; the High Church (catholic) view— supported in general by the Prayer Book—was that when baptized a person was reborn immediately into the life of Christ. As Newman gradually slipped from the restraints of the evangelicalism in which he had been reared, this cardinal doctrine assumed a central place in his thinking, and he gave to it hard, sustained thought. Initially, he believed that "the great stand is to be made, *not* against those who connect a spiritual change with baptism, but those who deny a spiritual change altogether."[116] The point was that spiritual regeneration was a gift of God and the spiritual test—indeed the test of salvation—came in what the baptized person did with the gift. Whether the gift was used or whether it atrophied, God, as the giver, would never take it away. For Newman, this interpretation was satisfying in that it did not diminish the mystery of God's salvific plan. The ineffability of baptismal regeneration was attractive to Newman because it meant that it stood beyond the reach of private judgment, outside the critical, subjective spirit that seemed to characterize the evangelical approach to salvation.

Eventually, Newman and the other Tractarians would inspire such a sharp divergence between themselves and the evangelicals over baptismal regeneration that the evangelicals would reject the doctrine altogether. Newman's gradual apprehension of the doctrine was in step with his measured acceptance of the visible Church. As we know, Newman's deliberate walk in this direction put him on the path that Keble and Pusey had been on since birth. Keble held up baptism above all other Church sacraments, and he expressed deep spiritual gratitude and took great personal delight in receiving infant children into Christ's Church. His poetic muse may not have been at its most eloquent when writing of baptizing children, but the sentiment was certainly sincere:

> O tender gem and full of Heaven!
> Not in the twilight stars on high,
> Not in moist flowers at even,
> See we our God so nigh.[117]

Newman expressed his mature Tractarian view on baptismal regeneration in *Lectures on the Doctrine of Justification,* published in 1838. His stated intention was to show that "certain essential truths, such as Baptismal Regeneration and the Apostolical Ministry" are not "incompatible with the doctrine of justifying faith."[118] Defining what constituted faith was central to Newman's project in these lectures. He was dismayed by the evangelicals' insistence on "preach[ing] conversion" rather than preaching Christ. The unhappy result of this skewed view of the Gospel was that "faith and . . . spiritual-mindedness are dwelt on as *ends,* and obstruct the view of Christ."[119] Newman argued that justification "is wrought by the power of the Spirit, or rather by His presence within us," while "faith and renewal are both present also, but as fruits of it."[120] Justification and renewal are "both included in that one great gift of God, the indwelling of Christ in the Christian soul."[121]

Newman strongly disagreed with Martin Luther's substitution of inward signs of grace for those of an outward nature and contemplation of self for reverence for the Church, as well as for having "professed to make the written word all in all," when in fact "he sacrificed it in its length and breadth to the doctrine which he had wrested from a few texts." Upon these selected texts the Protestant preacher ruminates to the exclusion of all else, Newman said. "Between true faith and self-contemplation, no wonder that where the thought of self obscures the thought of God, prayer and praise languish, and only preaching flourishes." For Newman, true faith was not something to be constantly brooded over. No, he argued, "true faith is what may be called colourless, like air or water; it is but the medium through which the soul sees

Christ; and the soul as little really rests upon it and contemplates it, as the eye can see the air."[122]

Newman's stand on baptismal regeneration was to see in it the justifying and renewing hand of God, regardless of the act of individual will. God's grace was imparted to the baptized child through the sacrament of the Church. Christ has bought admission to the heavenly kingdom through his shed blood whether or not such is ever admitted by the recipient. The life of faith comes after baptism. The duty to improve in faithfulness remains, although some do not fulfill this duty. Therefore, the Protestant (Calvinist) distinction between saint and sinner, between regenerate and unregenerate, was to Newman *unreal,* although a detested Noetic Edward Hawkins, Newman's one-time Oriel colleague, had once got such a distinction about right in Newman's view: "Religious and moral excellence is a matter of degree. Men are not either saints or sinners; but they are not so good as they should be, and better than they might be,—more or less converted to God."[123]

The three leading Tractarians were in accord over the cardinal issue of baptismal regeneration. And as their position and agreement solidified through the 1830s so, too, did their opposition to any and all who rejected this doctrine. Their high view of baptism was tested occasionally in a practical manner, such as in 1834 when a sometime St. Mary's parishioner by the name of Jubber, a Baptist, requested that Newman marry his daughter. The daughter was unbaptized, and Newman refused on the grounds that she was an "outcast" from the Church and therefore needed to be baptized before he could in good conscience perform the wedding ceremony. Richard Bagot, bishop of Oxford, was mindful of Newman's principled stand based on the Prayer Book rubric; but at a time when the Church's exclusive control of marriage was under attack by the parliamentary Whigs, he would have preferred Newman to have married the woman and spared the Church the sarcastic volleys from the politicians and the press, which came in due course.[124] Nevertheless, Newman refused to perform the ceremony.

Keble and Pusey supported fully Newman's controversial action. "I trust it will do good through evil report and good report," wrote Pusey.[125] And Keble commended Newman for "a distinct and conscientious protest against one of our crying grievances."[126] A couple of years later, in 1836, the Melbourne government introduced a civil marriage bill, which when passed by Parliament, ended the Church's exclusive control of the social institution. But Newman had made his stand that the Church was not subservient to the state—in this matter at least—and that he had acted according to its own higher law.

The Jubber episode is suggestive of the kind of popular criticism the Tractarians attracted. Criticism of a higher theological nature came by way of the evangelicals and from churchmen concerned with the "Romanizing" tendency of Tractarian teaching. The evangelicals expressed little opposition to the Tractarians during the initial years of the Movement. The latter's stress on the apostolic succession was extreme, thought most, but the doctrine itself was not in dispute. The Tractarians' belief in baptismal regeneration also elicited considerable opposition, but it took the combination of the publication of Hurrell Froude's incendiary *Remains* in 1838, the growing prominence in the Movement of harsh critics of the Church of England such as W. G. Ward and Frederick Oakeley, and the appearance of Newman's *Tract 90* in 1841 to make the evangelicals denounce them completely.[127]

Evangelicals thought that the Tractarians gave too much importance to the church fathers. The Tractarians championed the church catholic, which in the view of evangelicals had become seriously corrupted and riddled with errors. And the Tractarians did not accord Scripture the preeminent place in the Christian religion evangelicals thought it merited. As the evangelical apologist William Goode phrased it in *The Divine Rule of Faith* (1842), the basic question was "whether in the testimony of the Fathers there is to be found anything which either in form or in substance we are bound to receive as the Word of God delivered to the Church by the apostles and consequently forming part of our Divinely-revealed Rule of faith and duty."[128] But in the opinion of the Tractarians, particularly Newman, the question had been answered already.

As the lines of division between the two parties hardened, the evangelicals engendered considerable internal unity by upholding the precepts of the Protestant Reformation against, as they saw it, the "papist" onslaught of the Tractarians. Reformation theology, with its strong emphasis on conversion became the central feature of evangelical theol-

ogy, and as a party evangelicals grew more suspicious of Church tradition, especially that having to do with ceremonial. The preexisting
similarities between evangelicals and Tractarians, well remarked upon in
the historiography of both movements, and also the evangelical family
background of some of the latter's leaders and adherents such as Newman and W. E. Gladstone, did not lead to much sympathy between
the two parties. Disaffection between them was chronic and was well-
personified by Pusey and Lord Shaftesbury, evangelicalism's parliamentary champion in the 1850s. These two regularly traded denunciations,
until Shaftesbury charged Pusey with religious "infidelity," whereupon
a pitched verbal battle erupted on the pages of London's *Morning Chron-
icle* in 1852. A tiresome, two-month correspondence between the religious combatants marked the occasion, most of which traded on the
currency of caricature.[129] No irenicon was visible here, or anywhere else,
at that time.

As the central twelve years of the Oxford Movement passed and
"Tractarianism" evolved into "Anglo-Catholicism" in the 1850s, theological concerns began to change. Pusey, reluctantly, it would seem, assumed the leadership of the Anglo-Catholics, and his chief concerns: the
Eucharist, ministry to the poor, and women's orders, came to characterize the social theology of the new generation of Tractarians. The recognition of a need for missions in Britain itself lay at the root of the Anglo-
Catholics' move into urban ministry.[130] Slum priests, especially in the
depressed East End of London, emerged as the personal instantiations
of Anglo-Catholic social engagement. They exhibited a zeal for soul-
saving that was almost evangelical in its earnestness, together with a
demonstrable interest in the physical condition of their parishioners and
a selflessness about their own well-being. William Bennett (1804–86)
became the archetypal slum priest, while serving at St. Barnabus', Pim-
lico, in the 1850s. The kind of service carried out by priests like Bennett
eventually helped to inspire the emergence of a new Tractarian social
dispensation in the last quarter of the nineteenth century.

While Tractarian theology bore Newman's broad imprint, we have
suggested that Pusey and Keble made important contributions of a particular nature, the effect of which was to sharpen certain features of the
Oxford Movement's theological message. The core elements of Tract-

arian theology—antiquity, the apostolic succession, baptismal regeneration, the Eucharist—each received an interpretation based on a new or, in some cases, a renewed sense of the Church and of catholic Christian tradition. The unchanging belief of the Tractarians that only in the early church could there be found the model for proper contemporary practice drove each of them to seek ancient guidance in formulating their religious orthopraxis and their theological orthodoxy. Both the journey and the results of this quest sustained the original Tractarian leaders (save Newman) within the Church of England, as it did many of their successors.

3 *Friendship*

*F*riendship was intrinsic to the Oxford Movement, and this chapter will examine it as a significant theme in Tractarian history. The friendships forged among the leading Tractarians were intense and deeply loyal.[1] As we shall see, they developed at different times and at different rates in the 1820s and 1830s, but together they formed the interpersonal foundation of the Movement. Like the archetypal Old Testament friendship of David and Jonathan, the friendships fashioned by the Tractarians were almost filial and highly emotional. This was especially true of Newman, who was shattered by Froude's death from tuberculosis in 1836. "I have this day," Newman lamented to a friend upon receiving word of Froude's passing, "heard tidings sadder to me on the whole than I ever can hear—i.e. more intimately and permanently trying, Froude's death. I never can have such a loss, for no one is there else in the whole world but he whom I could look forward to as a contabernalis for my whole life."[2]

Friendship gave to the Oxford men a camaraderie, a sense of common cause and team unity which produced a feeling of invincibility and rightness. The Tractarians were friends as well as allies; they were a band of brothers. And from their radical and fraternal position at Oriel

College they launched their attack on the apparent apostasy and Erastianism of the times.

As we noted in Chapter 1, the Oriel College common room was Oxford University's most intellectually vibrant in the 1820s and 1830s. In these last years before the railway arrived in the ancient university city, student and scholar alike resided in a gilded place as yet almost untouched by the industrial revolution raging around it. Oriel was by no means the most architecturally prepossessing of the colleges; that honor usually went to Christ Church. Nor did its gardens offer much to admire when compared with the glory of Trinity's, where Newman had been an undergraduate. But in the composition of its fellowship, and in its intellectual thrust and parry, Oriel stood out. Despite Oxford's placid face, its famous "dreaming spires," the university had undergone its own revolution, in education, around 1800—a rejection of eighteenth-century academic apathy—which led to a more systematic approach to teaching and examining. At Oriel, three successive provosts—John Eveleigh, Edward Copleston, and Edward Hawkins—took these educational reforms very seriously and pushed the college to the forefront of the university. Oriel's undergraduates were selected carefully, tutors took their jobs seriously, and college fellowships were open to general and stiff competition.

All the principal participants in the Oxford Movement were fellows of Oriel. Keble, Newman, Froude, and Pusey had all passed Oriel's grueling week-long fellowship examination. And during their time as college fellows they (with the exception of Pusey, who remained at Oriel only a short time, 1823–28) gradually coalesced as both colleagues and friends. Oriel was the base for their project of Church revival and social renewal. The Movement worked outward from the college, and the friendships established there sustained it in its early, hectic years. But the passing of time and the alteration of views brought an end to these fraternal links even while other such like-minded clusters of friends were established later on and in other places.

John Keble, the eldest of the Tractarians, was born in 1792 and went up to Oxford—to Corpus Christi College—in 1807, when he was not quite fifteen years old. As his best biographer, Georgina Battiscombe, observes: "In Keble's day a young man was sent to Oxford or Cambridge

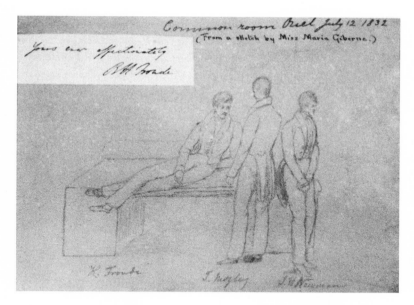

Richard Hurrell Froude, John Henry Newman, and James Mozley in Oriel Common Room. *From an 1832 sketch by Miss Maria Giberne. Froude, the most provocative of the Tractarians, urged Newman to become more radical in his religious stance. Upon his early death four years later, Newman was almost inconsolable. By permission of the Provost and Fellows of Oriel College, Oxford.*

to be confirmed in the tradition in which he had been brought up rather than to gain an understanding of other and alien traditions."[3] And such was certainly the case for the retiring youth from Fairford vicarage in Gloucestershire. Here Keble had grown up under the steady paternal hand of John Keble, senior, a churchman of the old High type, thoroughly committed to a right reading of Anglican catholicity and to the maintenance of the religio-political establishment. Though shy, the younger Keble was exceptionally intelligent; and his Oxford Bachelor of Arts degree, which he took in 1810, was adorned with a double first in mathematics and classics. In the spring of 1811 he was elected to a fellowship at Oriel. He was just nineteen.

In joining the Oriel common room Keble was entering an exclusive world of academic privilege, rarefied conversation, and social prestige. Most Oxford senior common rooms at this time still remained "comfortably reminiscent of a cathedral close," as Battiscombe notes.[4] But Oriel was not among them, and Keble in fact did not care for the intellectually combative tenor of the place. Oriel was fast gaining a reputation for intellectual daring and questioning—the seedbed of the Noetics' contrarianism, that group of dons who thrived on a diet of spirited debate and controversy—and Keble wanted none of it. His formative years, spent in "the sacred seclusion of English family life,"[5] as the future Tractarian Tom Mozley characterized Keble's upbringing, precluded any desire to participate in the verbal to and fro of the Oriel common room.

In his early years at Oriel Keble occupied himself with considerable reading and essay writing, carrying out the work for which he had been named a fellow in characteristic quietude and modesty. His essays won university prizes for English and Latin in 1812, and a few years later in 1818 he became a college tutor. Keble saw his tutorial role as mostly pastoral and concerned himself more with the moral development of his pupils than their intellectual. He also became a deacon and in turn was ordained, and this natural ministerial progression reinforced his commitment to the essentially clerical nature of his vocational tasks. "You consider tuition a species of pastoral care, do you not?" he asked John Coleridge, his close friend from undergraduate days at Corpus Christi and the nephew of the poet, Samuel Taylor Coleridge, "otherwise it might seem questionable whether a clergyman ought to leave a cure of souls for it. And yet there are some people in Oxford who seem to imagine that College Tutors have nothing to do with morale."[6] The stance of some of his colleagues at Oriel was the intended target of this mild barb. But the interpretation Keble gave to his job as tutor was one that would eventually greatly influence Newman and Froude once they, too, became Oriel tutors.

Keble's concern for his pupils' moral development did not lead him to extremes of preaching and hectoring, however, things for which the evangelicals had a reputation. He abhorred evangelicalism and distanced himself from colleagues with any trace of it in their spiritual makeup. As Newman later recalled, his own evangelical beginnings had left their mark on him, and as a consequence Keble "fought shy" of the younger man in the early days of their acquaintance.[7] Keble's temperament was moderate, and he was deeply conservative in his religiosity, shrinking from speaking of the holy and essential features of his faith. He was well practiced in reserve, as was his devout father. Though naturally unassuming, Keble's modesty effected its own attraction, and undergraduates were drawn to him. And given his youth and outlook, Keble usually found them more congenial than many of the older members of the Oriel common room.

From about 1818 to 1823, Keble became a well-known and a well-respected member of the university. Newman arrived as an undergraduate in Oxford in 1817 and recognized Keble's saintly and friendly character early on, as did Pusey, who was the third of the future Tractarians to become a fellow of Oriel (in 1823). However, Froude was the first of the group of three with whom Keble felt a real bond.

Richard Hurrell Froude, born in 1803, was eleven years younger than Keble. The eldest son of a well-known Anglican archdeacon, Robert Hurrell Froude, Hurrell, as the son was called, went up to Oriel in 1821. Keble became his tutor. At first, Froude's naturally outspoken and eager manner caused the sensitive Keble to withdraw. But not for long, as the irrepressible Froude found a way to capture Keble's sympathy and imagination. The friendship was two years in gestation, only beginning really in 1823, the year that Keble resigned his Oriel fellowship and took up a curacy at Southrop in Gloucestershire. Keble was overjoyed to be returning to his rural roots, escaping the relative excitement of Oxford. During the long summer vacation, he invited Froude and two other undergraduates, Robert Wilberforce and Isaac Williams, to come to Southrop as part of an extended reading party. Here in the dreamy atmosphere of high summer the group concentrated on reading Aristotle and the classic poets. During this idyll, Froude became very impressed by Keble's devotion to spirituality and the nurturing of virtue. In this manner he reminded Froude of his mother, Margaret, who had died the previous year and would be forever memorialized by an adoring son: "I think the more I see of him I get to like and admire him more [*sic*]; in everything but person and manner he seems so very like my mother," he wrote to his father the archdeacon.[8]

Keble's view of Froude was likewise laudatory, though the older man's sobriety was not reflected in his youthful charge. Froude's quick and clever mind needed tempering, thought Keble. Religion and the life of devotion required a certain degree of seriousness that precluded quick answers and trite observations. As Keble said in a gentle rebuke to Froude prior to the latter's returning to Oxford at the end of the summer: "You said one day Law's *Serious Call* was a clever book; it seemed to me as if you had said that the Day of Judgement would be a pretty sight."[9]

Once back at Oriel Froude began preparing for his final examinations, which would come in the autumn of 1824. His aim was the vaunted double first achieved by his mentor Keble, and he worked extremely hard, even through a bout with smallpox, to take Oxford's highest undergraduate honor. But he failed, taking only a second-class degree. However, like Newman, Froude did not let examination failure keep him from trying for an Oriel fellowship. For the next year and a half he occupied himself with studying and teaching. He also took an important trip with Keble to the ruins of Tintern Abbey, which did much to bring together in his mind religion, romance, and medievalism, some of the themes of the summer reading party and characteristic of Keble's thinking. It was here on the sylvan banks of the River Wye that Froude's later fierce attraction to catholic traditions was fired. A few months later in 1826 he tried Oriel's fellowship examination and was duly elected, another blow to the "quackery of the schools,"[10] as Provost Copleston called Oxford's unimaginative examination system, which he thought, while a revealing test, was not the only way to judge academic talent.

Surprisingly, Froude's initial period as a fellow of Oriel was marked by a reticence similar to that displayed by Newman a few years earlier and by Keble earlier still. For Froude, however, his reticence was brought on by a severe spiritual crisis during 1826–27, the nature of which has been contested by historians and biographers ever since Geoffrey Faber published *Oxford Apostles: A Character Study of the Oxford Movement* in 1933.[11] Faber contended that homosexual desire lay at the root of Froude's crisis, and his way out of this moral morass was to sublimate his sexual appetite to a transforming ideal. As Faber explains it, "A negative abstinence was not enough. Only a positive ideal could subdue the beast within him. The idea of virginity fulfilled this function as nothing else could."

In advancing this ideal no one was more important than Newman, whose own supposed struggle with repressed homosexuality Faber comments upon.[12] Newman dispensed with the idea of marriage for himself in the late 1820s, remarking that "the virginity of the Christian soul is marriage with Christ."[13] For both men the way forward lay in a self-denying celibacy.

Critics of Faber's view of Froude have been many. Most notably, his biographer Piers Brendon argues that "it was aspects of Romanticism rather than latent homosexuality" that Froude sought to sublimate in celibacy and a course of self-denial, fasting, and deprivation the extremes of which became public when his private journal was published posthumously in 1838.[14] Newman attributed to Froude "a high severe idea of the intrinsic excellence of virginity," and neither virginity nor celibacy were ever far from the guiding path created for Tractarianism by Newman and Froude.[15] Both Keble and Pusey, however, married, much to Newman's disappointment.[16]

By the spring of 1827 Froude seems to have put behind him the acuteness of the crisis, whatever its genesis. He had been gradually cultivating a catholic spirituality, and his growing admiration for some Roman Catholic practices such as celibacy and sacramentalism and a concomitant strong view of the Church caused some among his friends to fear that a Roman conversion was alarmingly imminent.[17] It was not, but Froude was beginning to develop the ideas that would help to form the foundation of the Oxford Movement.

Meanwhile, Keble, long a practitioner of catholic spirituality and Froude's chief mentor in this regard, was busy composing the poetry that would result in *The Christian Year*.[18] This work of High Anglican religiosity was an early literary representation of the Oxford Movement. Typically, Keble was skeptical of its worth: "It will be still-born, I know very well," he told Isaac Williams, another of the Oriel group.[19] He was wrong. Keble's thin volume of poetry was immediately popular and sold well. *The Christian Year* also reawakened institutional Oxford to someone who had departed from the place four years before and had not been much on the scene since. Of course, Keble was not concerned about his standing in Oxford now, having given himself over wholly to the life of a country vicar, but there were those who did wonder at the prospect of

Keble's return. Froude was chief among them; and when Oriel's provostship came open in 1827 upon Copleston's elevation to the see of Llan-
daff, he campaigned vigorously for the election of his mentor. Froude
was loudly confident that if Keble became provost he "would bring in
with him quite a new world, that donnishness and humbug would be
no more in the College, nor the pride of talent, nor an ignoble secular
ambition."[20] Keble was not opposed to the possibility of becoming provost, but characteristically he was not the least inclined to fight for sufficient support from the fellows when it became clear that another
member of the common room, Edward Hawkins, was also in the run-
ning for the post. Keble withdrew from the contest on the grounds that
such a competition would cause disunion in the college, and Hawkins
was elected unanimously in early 1828. A few years later in 1831 Keble
happily was elected as Oxford's Professor of Poetry in a unanimous vote,
a part-time post which allowed him to remain in the country.

The beginning of Hawkins's provostship marks an important stage
in the gestation of the Oxford Movement, for it was under his tenure
that the Oriel common room became the intensely divisive place that
sealed its fame and helped form the Tractarians. The year 1828 also
marked the start of a great intensification of national political affairs that
challenged severely Keble's essentially passive nature, which until then
had seen him content to leave the hotly contested world of politics "in
the hands of our Governors and to find as little fault with them as I can.
This," he said portentously, "I take to be true Toryism."[21] Roman Catholic emancipation, the first great political challenge to the early ideals of
the Oxford Movement, was stirring and would come to full flower in
1829, as we have seen in our treatment of politics in Chapter 1. This
issue would be the one around which the nascent Tractarians would first
gather intellectually, and it would go far in awakening them to the cardinal features of church and state as they stood in the last years of Regency
England.

During the late 1820s Froude moved out of Keble's immediate
orbit and cemented his friendship with Newman during the college's
budding tutorship controversy. Their joint opposition to Oriel's existing
system of common tutorials and the lack of pastoral concern exhibited
by many college tutors bound them together in common cause. As was

suggested earlier, Keble's example was pronounced in this affair. In the battle with Provost Hawkins over tutorial style some of the main themes of the Oxford Movement were rehearsed. Adding to this rehearsal was the spirited opposition to Peel's support of Catholic emancipation and the apparent attack on the Anglican establishment that such a position entailed. The "apostolicals," as Newman and Froude had begun to call themselves in reference to their faith in the example of the early church, forged an even deeper bond through the political coming-out engendered by their denunciation of Peel and their successful campaign to see the anti-emancipationist, Sir Robert Inglis, elected as burgess for the university in 1829. Newman was ecstatic at the "glorious victory" in "the first public event I have been concerned in."[22]

The bond between Newman and Froude deepened over the next three years. The two became inseparable, and their unity was strengthened further by the advent of the agitation over the Reform Bill in 1831, which was designed to widen the parliamentary franchise to the benefit of Dissenters. Once again, the Oxford men saw the Church's prerogatives under attack. They denounced the bill and vilified its parliamentary supporters. The Whig ministry was to blame for this outrage, this strike against the confessional state, they argued. Newman called its conduct "atrocious."[23] Froude's radical nature easily took him further, to the point of advocating the separation of church and state so as to end finally the Whigs' meddling in the sacred affairs of the Church.[24] Even Keble was similarly exercised and in a letter to a friend in 1832 referred sarcastically to King William IV's realm as the "republican State of England."[25] Nevertheless, disestablishment always remained too extreme a course for Keble, although not for the highly emotional Froude.

Events conspired to drive the Oxford men even closer together. As we noted in Chapter 1, early in 1833, not long after the passage of the Reform Bill, the Whig government introduced a bill to suppress ten Irish bishoprics and use their endowments in the service of the remaining ones, or for other purposes yet to be determined. Fiscally, the move made sense; the bishoprics were in fact redundant. However, Newman, Froude, and Keble did not see matters in this mundane way. Rather, once again, they saw the Church as under assault by an irreligious government. The Irish Church Temporalities Bill, which Newman would shortly brand the "Sacrilege Bill," confirmed for them the parlous position of the Church.[26] Outrage was a constant state of mind, especially for Newman and Froude. They were "united in a chivalric comradeship,"[27] as Brendon calls their friendship, which yielded also a great concern for Froude's delicate health. His worsening tuberculosis, the bane of many nineteenth-century young people, demanded attention, and so the two Oriel dons, together with Froude's father, decided to escape oppressively Erastian England in December 1832 and travel to the Mediterranean for a restorative interlude.

This trip is justly famous in the history of the Oxford Movement, for it was during the group's sojourn through Gibralter, Greece, Corfu, Malta, Sicily, and Italy that Froude and Newman began to see a larger purpose in their opposition to the Erastianism into which, in their view, the Church of England had slipped. The trip proved highly instructive and steadily enlightening. The Greek Orthodox Church and the Roman Catholic Church were viewed *in situ*. Local clergy and their congregations were observed going about their normal tasks. Initially, neither one greatly impressed the two Oxonians. Froude, characteristically, was blunt in his denunciation of Malta as a "land of superstition."[28] Newman wrote to his sister Harriett that the Greek clergy were "of the lower rank . . . very ignorant but moral in their lives."[29] The Italian clergy and people were likewise found wanting. In Naples, again reporting to Harriett, Newman assessed the Roman Catholic population as "immersed in the most despicable frivolity and worst profligacy, which is so much connected with religious observances as to give the city the character of a pagan worship."[30]

Newman and the Froudes then proceeded on to Rome. Unsurprisingly, the eternal city floored them: "The effect of every part is so vast and overpowering,"[31] Newman enthused in a letter to a friend, and so some time was required in order to absorb intellectually and esthetically the seat of Roman Catholic power and the former center of the Roman Empire. Froude's assessment, however, was no more laudatory than that given to the Maltese. He dismissed the Catholics of Rome as "idolators."[32] Such a description reflected the usual prejudices displayed by nineteenth-century Englishmen. Naturally, Froude's position was theologically nuanced in a way that much surpassed the popular anti-Catholicism of most of his countrymen. But it was the blatant Erastianism, the sheer irreligious social accommodation of the Roman Catholic Church in southern Italy, that really appalled him. Newman, too, found much about the Roman Church that dismayed him, but also much that he found strangely attractive. He believed that high catholic principles had been corrupted over time. "Dead flies cause the precious ointment to stink," he lamented in a letter to Henry Jenkyns, a sympathetic Oriel fellow.[33]

The Froudes and Newman included the Catholic English College in their tour of Rome. Its rector was Nicholas Wiseman, later to play an indispensable role in the growth of the Roman Catholic Church in England. Froude and Newman were impressed personally with Wiseman but not with his clearly held position that the Church of England and the Church of Rome could not hope for a closer relationship unless the former accepted the provisions of the Council of Trent, to include the doctrine of papal ascendancy. Froude was greatly disappointed with Wiseman's entrenched position, remarking bitterly that the Roman Catholic clergy were "wretched Tridentines everywhere."[34]

Newman was less annoyed and perhaps more inspired by the obstacle of Trent than his traveling companion. When encouraged by Wiseman to make another visit to Rome, Newman replied solemnly and prophetically: "We have a work to do in England."[35] Froude, however, and for different reasons, was more anxious to return straightway to England than was Newman, who decided to prolong his trip by journeying back to Sicily. The Froudes, father and son, attempted to dissuade Newman from remaining behind, but he was set on concluding his time abroad with some time alone. They parted, amicably, in April, and Newman proceeded on to Sicily. Physically, the last portion of his continental excursion was extremely trying, as he fell ill, probably with typhoid fever. But spiritually, Newman's last days before a most welcome return to England, and to "work," were full and empowering as his disposition toward the local Sicilians improved and his apprehension of their Church softened. When at last he departed for France, the boat on which he had booked passage soon found itself languishing in the doldrums for a week. And it was during this enforced wait in the Mediterranean's Straits of Bonifacio that the vexatious Newman was inspired to write the poem that opened with the words "Lead, kindly light, amid the encircling gloom." This poem reinforced his belief in trusting faith and the revealed Church and would later become his most famous hymn, "The Pillar of the Cloud." Finally, on July 8, 1833, he reached England, arriving home in Oxford the next day. Five days later, on July 14, Keble ascended the pulpit at St. Mary's, Oxford, the University Church, and preached his Assize sermon on national apostasy. The Oxford Movement's public phase had begun.

Froude's return to Oxford had occurred a month before Newman's and had come after an enlightening passage through France. His time there had awakened him to the ideas of F. R. de Lamennais, an advocate of disestablishment, whose movement in France was based on Church independence and radical republican enfranchisement, which would, he thought, broaden the influence of the French Church among the general population.[36] Froude's energy thus became directed at reviving the catholic, apostolic, and independent idea of the Church of England by using Lamennais's ideas as a model. As we have seen, Froude had no time for what he considered the bloated and misguided papal system. But the history of the Roman Church, combined with the populism of Lamennais's movement and the constant depredations of the parliamentary Whigs, had enlivened and enlarged his imagination concerning the essential catholicity of the Church of England. He began to talk of promulgating this message in "short tracts and letters."[37] The Church of England must be revived! It must shed the dead weight of Erastianism! It must better reflect catholic tradition! It needs to have greater appeal to the people! Froude was going off in all directions. And then fortuitously for Froude, Newman returned in a state of mind similar to that of his excited friend.

Keble, too, shared this state of mind, but his characteristic reserve made his preaching on England's "apostasy" on July 14 less dramatic than Newman would have us believe when he wrote later that "I have ever considered and kept the day, as the start of the religious movement of 1833."[38] Nevertheless, Keble's relatively impassioned sermon denouncing the state's incursions into the domain of the Church did give a focus and an urgency to the course the Oxford men were now adopting. And their mutual friendship bound them together in a tight circle. As Sheridan Gilley remarks accurately: "The heart of the Oxford Movement was just this, the personal loyalty and affection between Newman, Froude and Keble, and their love and affection for Oxford."[39]

But as has been suggested earlier, Keble's apprehension of the Church's predicament had been reached via a lifetime's devotion to and understanding of the catholic and apostolic nature of the Church of England, whereas Froude and Newman had just become aware of the Church's essential claims to these things. Newman's Mediterranean wanderings and his spiritual reverie amid a cargo of oranges on the slow boat from Italy to France had confirmed for him the Church's real nature. Likewise, Froude's new understanding had been strengthened by his exposure to Lamennais in France. Clearly there was something of the excitement of the new convert in Newman and Froude's electric response to their sunny southern interlude. Keble exhibited passion, too, but his was not that of the revelatory kind, but rather that of the gratification that comes with the emergence of a long-held belief into the clear light of day. The three friends were ready to make common cause in the name of the Church, but their angles of approach differed. Their shared base was Oriel, but not all the members of its common room were ready to support this apostolic project. What can be found if the collegiate epicenter of the newly launched Oxford Movement is probed?

Robin Sharwood, in an important essay published to mark the 150th anniversary of the beginning of the Oxford Movement, dissects the composition of the Oriel common room as it stood in 1833. As we know, the Noetics, the "old Oriel school," greatly resisted the ideas of Newman, Froude, and Keble. Led by Provost Edward Hawkins, the Noetics thought the "apostolicals" gravely mistaken on the major issues facing church and state. But even more, it was the ethos of catholic piety and pastoral care that irritated the worldly and contemporary Noetics. These "march-of-mind" men, as Newman called them disparagingly, resisted the attempt to remake Oriel.[40] They were openly critical of the influence of the trio, according to Sharwood, and were quite content to range themselves in opposition to the nascent Tractarians.[41]

In 1833, by Sharwood's count, there were fourteen Oriel fellows in addition to Newman, Froude, and Keble.[42] Five or six members of the common room supported the Tractarian trio, while four were opposed.

Four fellows were uninvolved.[43] (To the Tractarian total can be added Edward Pusey who had migrated from Oriel back to his undergraduate home of Christ Church, as Regius Professor of Hebrew. His importance to the Movement would only increase.)

The Oriel base of the three friends was therefore a strong one but it was not static. Newman, in particular, used it unceasingly for most of the ten years after 1833 to forge the Movement and deepen the mutual commitment the Tractarians had one to another. But Oriel gradually lost its central position in the Movement as both Keble—already living in the country—and Froude—who would seek the warmth of Barbados on account of his health in late 1833—departed. Only Newman remained, but his entrenchment was disproportionately deep as both college fellow and as vicar of St. Mary's.

Close by, however, was Edward Pusey. His friendship with the others was slower to grow but it was vital to the development of the Movement. In 1828, Pusey gave up his Oriel fellowship to become Regius Professor of Hebrew and canon of Christ Church and thus return to his undergraduate college where he would now spend the rest of his long life. Pusey was from a minor aristocratic family, and his father was staunchly High Church. He was a meticulous scholar, and during the 1820s while an Oriel fellow he devoted considerable time and travel to studying German theology and learning the German language, which resulted in the weighty tome *Theology of Germany,* published in 1828. Pusey's early devotion to scholarship led him, in the view of Colin Matthew, to a position of political liberalism and theological latitudinarianism, of which his book on German theology provides ample evidence.[44] The book's critical reviewers rightly deemed it to be a liberal work, and this both shocked the apparently naïve Pusey and drove him back to the high churchmanship of hearth and home in the early 1830s, to which he remained loyal for the remainder of his eighty-two years.

Pusey's youthful liberalism came at the same time that Newman, Keble, and Froude were beginning to form the basis of the Oxford Movement. Pusey was not a close friend of any of the three until the late 1820s, at which time he began to cultivate relationships with these men, whom he now recognized as essentially like-minded. He was slow in aligning himself publicly with the Movement after its formal begin-

ning in the summer of 1833 because of his wariness toward innovation
of any sort, made plain by what he considered now to have been a
mistaken foray into German theology. But the publication of the *Tracts
for the Times* in September 1833 captured Pusey's imagination; and once
the *Tracts* had proved themselves, he decided to make a scholarly contribution to the series two years later. He wrote three long treatises on the
sacrament of baptism, as we saw in Chapter 2, which had the effect of
deepening the scholarship of the tracts and making them more serious
theological works. Pusey's tracts also had the very welcome outcome of
giving to the Movement, in Newman's words, "a front to the world . . .
he was able to give a name, a form, and a personality, to what was
without him a sort of mob."[45] Pusey, the aristocratic professor and cathedral canon, supplied a scholarly depth and a social imprimatur that did
much to legitimize the fledging movement. Indeed, so great was Pusey's
impact that the Movement came to be called Puseyism by some, although the title often was used pejoratively.

Pusey's late arrival on the Tractarian scene almost coincided with
Froude's removal from the center of the action, first by his health hiatus
in Barbados and then finally by his early death in 1836. Froude sailed for
Barbados in November 1833, where he took up residence at Codrington
College, a Church of England foundation near Bridgetown. There
Froude became a rather prickly chaplain to the first bishop of Barbados,
William Coleridge, a High Churchman of the old and therefore suspicious "Z" variety, and then later a rather dissatisfied college mathematics
instructor. Froude corresponded frequently with the other Tractarians
while attempting to slow down the raging bacillus that was killing him.
He wrote feverishly in the pages of his journal, composed a few tracts
and essays, and encouraged Newman in particular on to greater heights
of catholicity. Despite the miraculous powers attributed to sunshine and
warm breezes by contemporary doctors, Froude arrived back in England
in May of 1835, no better than when he had left a year and a half before.

Froude's health declined steadily. He died in February 1836, not
quite thirty-three years old. Keble was devastated, Newman, as we know,
disconsolate. "I have just had one of the greatest losses I can have in this
world the loss of my dear friend Froude," Newman wrote to a friend.[46]
The blow was both personal and corporate. The Movement had been at

the center of Froude's intellectual and spiritual existence, and Newman wanted this known to the wider world. Newman consulted Keble about what to do to bring this about, and the two decided to edit and publish Froude's private journals as a memorial to their dead friend. This decision was not taken lightly. As the two editors readily acknowledged in the preface to the *Remains,* as the publication was called: "It is in itself painful, nay revolting, to expose to the common gaze papers only intended for a single correspondent."[47] Froude's passionate commitment to the catholic revivalist goals of the Movement was never less than clear throughout the text, and Newman and Keble sought to prepare readers for what they were about to encounter by describing Froude's position thus: "The view which the Author would take of his own position was probably this; that he was a minister not of any human *establishment,* but of the one Holy Church Catholic . . . in England."[48]

The *Remains* came out in two volumes in 1838–39. Froude's listing of the ascetic practices he had maintained as a personal regimen to attain holiness seemed new, strange, and even comic to many readers: "Slept on the floor," Froude had recorded in the autumn of 1826. "Tasted nothing today till tea time, & then only one cup, & dry bread."[49] His outbursts against the government, however, might have been expected: "If it was not for a personal hatred of the Whigs, I should care comparatively little for the Reform Bill. For the Church can never right itself without a blow up,"[50] he wrote in 1831. But Froude's violent intolerance of the Protestant Reformation and his praising of Roman Catholicism were what really stirred up opposition to what the *Remains* seemed to say about the Movement. In an 1834 denunciation that soon became infamous among evangelicals and famous among churchmen, he wrote: "Really I hate the Reformation and the Reformers more and more."[51]

But there was worse to come: "The Reformation was a limb badly set—it must be broken again in order to be righted."[52] "I am afraid I must confess that the only war I could enter into with spirit, would be a civil war."[53] "Catholic enthusiasts may be hated, but they never can become as ridiculous as the Methodists are."[54] Froude's posthumous writings radicalized the Oxford Movement and scandalized its opponents, and not a few of its own supporters. After 1838, neutrality was impossible, and the Movement's catholic bias was now clear for all to see. Newman was prepared for "a flood of criticism, and from all quarters,"[55] he wrote to his old and trusted Trinity friend John Bowden. And he got it. The dam broke, and Newman and Keble faced a torrent of abuse and mockery over the impassioned writings of their deceased friend. But such a jolt was not altogether unwelcome to the two men, nor was it to Pusey, because it spoke of a deepening collective catholicism and a willingness to make plain their commitment to it as the basis for a renewed Church of England. With the publication of the *Remains* a new phase of the Movement had begun.

Indeed, the mid-late 1830s marked the apogee of the Movement. Despite the continuing bereavement over the loss of Froude, the remaining Tractarians were intent on making a deep impact on Oxford and on the Church of England altogether. The *Tracts for the Times* continued to roll off the press, and would do so until 1841. Newman assumed the editorship of the *British Critic* in 1838, completing the transformation of this old High Church journal into a Tractarian magazine. Its pages became filled with the exhortations of Tractarians and sympathizers. Newman's weekly sermons at St. Mary's attracted and captivated large numbers of people, especially undergraduates.[56] The poet Matthew Arnold's famous remembrance captures well the homiletic magic practiced by Newman from the pulpit of the University Church: "Who could resist the charm of that spiritual apparition, gliding in the dim afternoon light through the aisles of St. Mary's rising into the pulpit and then, in the most entrancing of voices, breaking the silence with words and thoughts which were a religious music—subtle, sweet, mournful?"[57]

Newman later remembered these years as "in a human point of view, the happiest time of my life."[58] And for Pusey, his early stirrings in trying to push the Movement in the direction of social responsibility are epitomized by his contribution of the very large sum of five thousand pounds in 1835 to the plan of the bishop of London, Charles Blomfield, for church-building in the depressed areas of the great metropolis.[59] Keble, meanwhile, remained comfortably ensconced in his new Hampshire living of Hursley, taken up in 1835, practicing his brand of pastoral Anglicanism and utterly content in the quietude of a rural parish.

Not all was light, however. The Tractarians had been collecting serious enemies since shortly after their trumpet call of July 14, 1833. In

1836, Thomas Arnold, father of the poet and the most famous school-master in English history, called them malignant in the *Edinburgh Review*.[60] His animus was based on the shoddy treatment given Renn Dickson Hampden by the Tractarians over his hotly contested appointment as Oxford's Regius Professor of Divinity in that year. This notable episode in Tractarian history is recounted in Chapter 4, but is useful here in pointing out the kind of enemies the Tractarians were making.

Newman was the least concerned of the Tractarian trio by the increased opposition the Movement was provoking. "In the spring of 1839," he recorded in the *Apologia*, "my position in the Anglican Church was at its height."[61] He took, it seems, a kind of sporting interest in provocation, but he had begun also to disengage gradually from the hurly-burly of Oxford by retreating more and more to the village of Littlemore, three miles out of town. As vicar of St. Mary's, Newman had taken a continuing interest in the suburban part of his parish since the early 1830s. From the cornerstone laid by his widowed mother, Jemima Newman, in 1835, a church rose and along with it a school. And as troubles increased in Oxford Newman began to seek the relative peace and quiet of Littlemore.

A particular source of trouble for the Tractarians as the 1830s drew to a close was Charles Golightly, a former pupil of Newman's whose disaffection for them had increased the more the Tractarians seemed publicly comfortable with Roman Catholicism. Froude's *Remains* had sealed Golightly's contempt for his former tutor and his equally deluded friends, and following its publication he launched a public campaign to raise funds for the building of an Oxford memorial to the English Protestant martyrs Nicholas Ridley, Thomas Cranmer, and Hugh Latimer. In so doing Golightly laid a small trap for the Tractarians: if they contributed to the memorial, then their deceased friend would be dishonored; if they refrained from contributing to it, then their "papist" inclinations would be confirmed.

Newman was both amused and annoyed by "goose Golightly and Co," he wrote to his sister Jemima.[62] Their frantic attempts to strike a blow against the Tractarians did result, in the end, in the construction of a dour, black memorial close by the Broad Street site where the three martyrs had been burnt at the stake at the command of the Catholic

Martyrs' Memorial, Oxford. Built by subscription in 1839, the monument to the English Protestant martyrs Ridley, Cranmer, and Latimer was meant to strike a blow against the Catholic sympathies of the Tractarians. Thomas Photos, Oxford.

Queen Mary in the 1550s.[63] The Tractarians chose not to contribute to Golightly's fund and weathered the Martyrs' Memorial storm, but a much greater one was brewing in the form of what would be the final installment of the *Tracts for the Times.*

For Newman, the storm took two years to break. During the summer of 1839 he was shaken by two realizations that changed utterly his thinking about the Church of England. As he later explained in the *Apologia:* "He who has seen a ghost can never be as if he had not seen it."[64] The first "ghost" came in the form of the Monophysites of the fifth century, a breakaway group of early Christians whose theology was deemed heretical by Rome. In reading their history Newman thought Anglicans to be in a similar position of schism. While the Church of England did not espouse the Monophysites' theology, which proclaimed a single, divine nature for Christ, their schismatic stance jolted him into the realization that in his view the Protestant Church of England was mirroring their rebellion.

The second "ghost" was supplied by an article in the August 1839 *Dublin Review,* titled the "Anglican Claim" and written by Nicholas Wiseman, now come back to haunt Newman some six years after their initial encounter in Rome. Wiseman's approach was to compare the African Donatist schismatics of the fourth century with contemporary Anglicans. Wiseman's argument hinged on the powerful words of St. Augustine: "Securus judicat orbis terrarum," the whole world judges surely. These words bore into Newman's mind, "the first real hit from Romanism that has happened to me," he called them.[65] Newman was shaken. "It has given me a stomach ache. . . . It does certainly come upon one that we are not at the bottom of things. At this moment we have sprung a leak."[66]

Newman's ultimate attempt to patch the "leak" came in the form of a tract published in 1841, two years after this epiphany. But before doing so he solidified his attachment to Littlemore by purchasing, along with a few friends, some land near the church upon which stood a former staging post for the old Oxford-Cambridge coach. Newman envisaged a monastic retreat house, and such is what Littlemore became for him from then until 1846.

Secure now in his Littlemore redoubt and moving quickly toward giving up the St. Mary's pulpit, Newman composed a defense of the Church of England's foundational Thirty-nine Articles so as to demonstrate their catholic soundness and to prove publicly Tractarianism's devotion to the Church. He had received little by way of encouragement in this endeavor from Keble, who thought that Wiseman's article was alarmist and not something that should vex Newman.[67] He did not see the need for a strong defense of the Church of England's raison d'être against such an attack. Newman, however, was clinging to his Anglican life and hoping to encourage others to do the same, especially some of the younger Tractarians, such as W. G. Ward and Frederick Oakeley, two Newman acolytes and catholic extremists who were pushing their leader to take the Movement in an even more overtly catholic direction.

The result was *Tract 90,* which appeared in February 1841. The theological position Newman took in the tract was hardly radical, however. His task had hardly been difficult. The Thirty-nine Articles could easily be made to bear a catholic interpretation. But the timing of Newman's tract was all wrong. Catholic-Protestant tensions in the Church were extraordinarily high, pushed to that position mainly by the Tractarians' own provocations. However, neither he nor Keble, who had begun to show more interest in the question and with whom Newman had consulted closely during the writing of the tract, pulled back from the abyss. Within two weeks, 2500 copies of this long (eighty-seven-page) and ponderous document were sold, and Newman's future in the English Church determined. "Our articles . . . are, through GOD'S good providence, to say the least, not uncatholic, and may be subscribed by those who aim at being catholic in heart and doctrine," wrote Newman moderately.[68] But almost nobody cared. No one, that is, whose devotion to the Church of England depended on a tortuous explication of its catholicity. Newman had erred in judgment severely and was about to feel the wrath of his erstwhile coreligionists.

Barely a week after *Tract 90* went into circulation, a group of opposing Oxford tutors wrote a letter calling upon the university authorities to take action against the tract and its presumed author, Newman. Shortly thereafter, Oxford's governing Hebdomadal Board decided to publicly censure *Tract 90.* Despite the swift harshness of the university's reaction Newman remained convinced of the necessity of his task and wrote Pusey to say that a "legitimate interpretation" of the Articles would stave off secessions from the Church, something with which the Tractarians now were grappling.[69] But the episode clearly took its toll on the embattled Newman. By the middle of March he told his faithful sister Harriett that he was "clean dished."[70] Then the bishop of Oxford, the ever-patient Richard Bagot, asked that the *Tracts* cease publication and that the offending *Tract 90* not be reprinted. Reluctantly, Newman complied with his bishop's decision.

Tract 90, however, was not the last controversy of 1841. That summer the Tractarians objected to the establishment of a by-definition heterodox bishopric in Jerusalem on a shared basis with the Lutherans and any other unattached Protestants in Palestine. Newman's reaction was much stronger than Keble's, however, and his growing disaffection for the Church of England was becoming clear to his closest friend. The year ended with Keble's expected retirement from the Poetry professorship and the launching of a campaign for the Oriel Tractarian Isaac Williams to fill the post. When it became clear that Williams's Tractarianism would prevent his election, he withdrew from the contest. Another defeat. As 1842 began the Oxford Movement was faltering.

Newman's fate, it seemed, was now sealed. But the working out of his final course of action took three years. As we have seen, from the summer of 1839 Newman's allegiance to the Church of England had been weakening gradually, and his vexation over ascending the St. Mary's and Littlemore pulpits on a weekly basis had become acute. As he explained to Keble: "What men learn from me, who learn anything, is to lean towards doctrines and practices which our Church does not sanction . . . I am in danger of acting as a traitor to that system."[71] Keble's allegiance to his Church was beyond question and therefore he could muster no sympathy for Newman's position, although he retained much sympathy for Newman's personal predicament.

As Newman struggled inwardly, Pusey brought the whole weight of university discipline down upon his own head by preaching a sermon in May 1843 in Christ Church Cathedral in which he upheld the Roman Catholic doctrine of the Real Presence in the Eucharist. The sermon was immediately branded heretical by Godfrey Faussett, the Lady Margaret Professor of Divinity and a strident foe of Tractarianism, and the complaint made its way to the university's vice-chancellor, Philip Wynter. A court of six doctors of divinity was convened, which included the anti-Tractarian Edward Hawkins from Oriel and the dyspeptic Faussett himself. Pusey's fate was clear from the fact that he was not allowed to speak in defense of his own position. From his Christ Church entrenchment Pusey refused to recant, and the court promptly suspended him from preaching in Oxford for two years.

While Oxford buzzed over Pusey's suspension, Newman's more private anguish was reaching its peak. In September 1843, he resigned from St. Mary's and, necessarily along with it, the Littlemore church. His last sermon as an Anglican was preached at Littlemore on the twenty-fifth of that month. In the sermon, known as "The Parting of Friends," Newman used well-known biblical stories of parting—such as David and Jonathan—to speak of the sundering of relationships now afflicting the Tractarian brotherhood spawned by college, Church, and shared beliefs.[72] Keble was at home in Hursley conducting his own service while Newman struggled through his Anglican memorial, but Pusey was there to conduct the Communion and to shed tears over the elements.[73]

Newman remained now in the quasi-monastery he had created for himself in the former coaching stables at Littlemore, and Pusey, though temporarily muzzled, assumed the leadership of the Movement. The next two years were dominated by the steady withering of Newman's commitment to the Church of England. This period was punctuated in 1844 by the publication of W. G. Ward's book, *The Ideal of a Christian Church,* which brought further opprobrium down on the Tractarians through his championing of the Roman Catholic Church and his crowing that "the whole cycle of Roman doctrine [is] gradually possessing numbers of English Churchmen."[74] The university responded by condemning the book and in a riotous gathering of Congregation at the Sheldonian Theatre degrading Ward from a Master of Arts to the status of an undergraduate.

Newman was deliberately oblivious to these penultimate acts in the Tractarian drama. Keble, similarly isolated at Hursley, was also insulated from the brunt of the events at Oxford. Only Pusey was on site to witness the spitefulness that the Oxford Movement had engendered within the university. And in part, the poisonous atmosphere of Oxford was responsible for spurring the export of the tenets of the Movement further afield. Keble and Pusey corresponded regularly throughout 1844 and 1845 over the best ways to extend Tractarian principles, including the revival of women's orders in the Church of England. But it was the "approaching parting," as Pusey lamented Newman's anticipated Roman conversion in a letter to Keble in the spring of 1845, that occupied much of his thinking. "I fear whenever it is, the rent in our poor Church will be terrible."[75]

The wait came to an end in October of that year. On the third of the month Newman instructed Edward Hawkins at Oriel to remove his name "from the books of the College and the University."[76] But despite the expectation of Newman's secession, news of its actual occurrence fell like a "thunderbolt" on Keble.[77] Newman was gone; his Anglican career, his Anglican life, was over. The friendship forged at Oriel was now, given the strength of competing convictions and the custom of the times, at an end. The news from Newman himself brought this sad reply from Keble: "You have been a kind and helpful friend to me in a way which scarce anyone else could have been . . . and yet I cannot go along with you. . . . May you have peace where you are gone, and help us in some way to get peace."[78]

Newman's response to Keble's farewell was equally poignant: "To you I owe it, humanly speaking, that I am what and where I am. . . . Let it be your comfort, when you are troubled, to think that there is one who feels that he owes all to you, who though, alas, now cut off from you, is a faithful assiduous friend unseen."[79]

The final parting with Pusey was cryptic, perhaps because of the intensity of the emotion shared at the Littlemore Church two years earlier. On the day before his conversion Newman wrote Pusey to say, "I trust he [Passionist priest Dominic Barberi] will receive me . . . into what I believe to be the one and only fold of the Redeemer."[80]

Newman's two closest friends had been left behind in his measured but determined departure for Rome. So, too, had the Movement that he and his long-deceased friend Froude had seen in vague prospect while traveling in Italy so many years before. The sundering of friendships had come to pass, but the Oxford Movement carried on with Pusey at the helm.

Within Oxford, Newman's departure left only Pusey and Charles Marriott, subdean of Oriel and appointed vicar of St. Mary's Church in 1850, to continue the Movement from positions of seniority. "No one," recalled Tom Mozley, Newman's brother-in-law, "sacrificed himself so entirely to the cause, giving to it all he had and all he was, as Charles Marriott."[81] But, in the pungent words of R. W. Church, "Oxford repudiated them." This repudiation encompassed Pusey, the devoted Marriott, and the larger Movement. "Henceforward," Church continues, "there was a badge affixed to them, and all who belonged to them, a badge of suspicion and discredit, and even shame, which made men beware of them."[82] Many of the younger men who had come under Newman's influence as undergraduates—such as Mark Pattison and James Anthony Froude, Hurrell's younger brother and the future historian—felt this disapprobation and soon became disillusioned with Tractarianism and migrated to the Broad Church or left the Church of England altogether.[83] The Oxford-centric Movement was at an end; friendship as it had been known and idealized had ceased.

Keble, unknowingly, symbolized the Oxford Movement's moving away from its center. Groups of "Tractarians," for such they were in temperament and ethos, formed in different places around the country.[84] Keble's own church, rectory, and parish became a beacon for those in search of the Tractarian message. But even more did the export of Tractarianism from Oxford find residence in the rapidly growing mid-Victorian towns and in the burgeoning metropolis of London.[85] Leeds became an important Tractarian outpost as Pusey worked hard to endow and establish St. Saviour's Church in the 1840s only to end up waging a titanic battle against W. F. Hook, then vicar of Leeds, whose own churchmanship ran counter to the Anglo-Catholicism originally envisaged for the church.[86] But in no place did there exist that spirit of reclamation, sport, and duty that had powered the original fraternal band at Oxford in the 1830s. The original battles had been fought; the original fighters had dispersed.

Still, during the late 1840s Keble and Pusey became as closely aligned personally as they had been during the heady days of the Movement. Battiscombe remarks that "the Oxford Movement might almost be regarded as the story of Keble's friendships."[87] And on the high plane of friendship Keble became Pusey's confessor in 1846. Such intimacy was sustaining as the two men fought for their interpretation of the Catholic Church of England against the Broad and the evangelical streams—and against the powerful tug exerted by the comfortable establishmentarianism so successfully depicted and satirized by Anthony Trollope in his "Barchester" novels of the period.

The high drama of Newman's secession and the impact it had on others who were greatly influenced by him and whose course of action was similar naturally caused the breaking of friendships and families beyond that of the Tractarian inner circle. The best-known example is that chronicled by David Newsome in *The Parting of Friends*.[88] In a reprise of Newman's sad and allusive sermon in 1843 at Littlemore, Newsome tells the story of the Wilberforce and Manning families, whose intimacy was riven by the crisis of faith centered on Roman Catholic secession.

As in any social movement friendship was central to the development of Tractarianism. The Oriel common room provided the physical and intellectual setting in which the leaders of the Oxford Movement could first coalesce and begin to form and then to forward their ideas. The feeling between Newman, Froude, Keble, and later, Pusey was intense even by the standards of the time. Their sense of camaraderie in what to them was an overwhelmingly good and necessary fight was the elixir that powered their relentless attack on a Church, and on a state and a society, that had, in their view, degraded its national religious practice in the name of liberalism and out of exigency. The agony of ultimate parting—first Froude's death and then Newman's secession—is what makes friendship within the Oxford Movement a sad and poignant feature of its history.

The last meeting of the three surviving friends took place at Hursley in 1865, the year before Keble's death. The few hours Newman, Keble, and Pusey spent together were a mixture of awkwardness and intimacy. For Newman and Keble, especially, the meeting—their first since Newman's conversion in 1845—reestablished the emotional bond rent twenty years earlier.[89] Nostalgia hung over them like a shroud. They were never to meet again, the two men whose friendship had begun when Newman, the painfully shy newest member of the Oriel fellowship in 1822, had been introduced to Keble and almost shrank from the seeming audacity of the moment.[90] But Oriel and all that it had meant to Newman stayed with him always. Across from his rooms at the Oratory in Birmingham, which he built and where he spent most of his Roman Catholic life, is the library. To stand in it is to stand in a smaller reproduction of Oriel's Senior Library. That is no coincidence.

4 *Society*
REVIVAL AND RECLAMATION

*T*he Oxford Movement's impact on Victorian British society was important, though uneven. Naturally, its political, religious, and theological features mark out its major boundaries. But to confine a study of the Movement to these cardinal features is to miss its wider social impact. The Tractarians, as we shall see, can never be mistaken for elaborate social thinkers. The hothouse atmosphere of industrial Britain engendered many prescriptions for the health of the nation. The "condition of England" question was on the lips of many, including the Tractarians. But none of them, with the qualified exception of Pusey, ever concerned themselves greatly with suggesting or mapping out ways to address the myriad social problems that beset the British nation during the most robust century of its history. The Tractarian prescription—if such it can be called—never included the increasing acceptance by society of state intervention in social welfare. For the men of Oxford, the Church was viewed as the repository of all that was necessary for the health of the nation, and to this position they clung while all around them the initiative for such work was taken by the state and by other agencies, religious and nonreligious alike.[1]

Nevertheless, the Tractarians did seek to ameliorate some of the social needs of the people in their society in ways that reflected their considered beliefs. This chapter will probe these in order to chart an identifiable Tractarian stance on social affairs from the 1830s to the 1870s. The poor, parish work, social action, women, laity, the Gothic Revival, and Gladstonian liberalism, all of these will be examined as areas in which the Tractarians forwarded a coherent social vision based on the primacy of the Church and an adherence to its principles of community, charity, and spirituality.

During the early years of the nineteenth century the new field of political economy was beginning to influence markedly public apprehensions of the proper ordering of British society. While secular thinkers such as David Ricardo, James Mill, and Jeremy Bentham were central to this development, the older traditions of Christian political economy remained strong nonetheless. The old school was best represented by the writings of Robert Malthus and John Bird Sumner, two Anglican clerics intensely interested in the practical concerns of population and economic wealth, and later by Edward Copleston, Richard Whately, and Thomas Chalmers. As the British state grappled with the challenges of severe inequities in wealth and a rapidly growing population,[2] the political economists—both Christian and secular—offered their assessments of the "condition of England" and what could be done about its worst features.

The Tractarians, like many others in contemporary society, were concerned especially about poverty and poor relief. In Georgian, Regency, and early Victorian Britain the clergy were taken seriously as commentators on social and economic affairs,[3] so it was natural for the Tractarians to be engaged by debates over British social conditions. The period of the French Revolutionary wars had made domestic instability a constant worry for the government. And the threat of revolution resulted in a number of state initiatives, including the introduction of a measure of outdoor relief for the poor, named Speenhamland after the place where it was devised, in 1795, which provided allowances for the poor based on the prevailing price of bread. Speenhamland was the most extensive government measure used to quell potential food riots—at the time the main yardstick of social disquiet—and its principle of parish-based relief was found in most parts of the realm, except in the far north and west. As a government measure, Speenhamland was politically conservative and economically modest and did not upset the Christian idea that true charity could flow only from the religious principle of caring for one's neighbor.

By the 1820s, in the aftermath of the Napoleonic period, Speenhamland and its accompanying Christian view of public welfare were coming under attack regularly by secular political economists, who found the position of the Christian political economists deeply problematic. The general population was rising rapidly; however, the percentage of that population in poverty was rising even more rapidly, and in the view of Ricardo and Mill, for example, the Church simply was overmatched as an agency of poor relief.[4]

In the wake of the significant constitutional changes of 1828–32, the way was opened for debate about other cardinal elements of the British domestic policy. As one of these, poor relief grew in importance as a topic of controversy both within and without Parliament. The Elizabethan Act of 1601 remained the cornerstone of the state's method of dealing with the downtrodden, and it hinged upon the principle of relief for those poor who were properly "settled" in the parish, a principle which had been reaffirmed by Speenhamland. However, as the Elizabethan law was well over two hundred years old, and since the ways in which individual parishes dealt with their resident poor went well beyond Speenhamland,[5] the critics of its present workings demanded and then got the establishment of the Poor Law Commission in 1832. An overhaul of poor relief ensued.

The Commission was charged with sorting out the jumble of poor relief methods that the thousands of parishes around the country used, and then with making recommendations for a new approach to combat the intractable problem of poverty. The Commission's nine members represented both the traditional school of Christian political economy and the expanding Ricardian school. Indeed, Peter Mandler argues that the widely held modern belief that the Poor Law Commission was an instrument of secular political economy is mistaken.[6] Christian theology was well represented at the Commission's table, and the finished product, the New Poor Law of 1834, was not a triumph of administrative reform or, as he observes, "the power of Benthamite ideas."[7] Poor relief did not, in 1834, suddenly become the preserve of technical prescription, divorced from older traditions of Christian charity. Relief would remain parish-based, and the importance of individual initiative was emphasized. Indeed, no one but the most blinkered could see a concession to human laziness and wanton carnality in the existence of the dismal workhouse, an institution with which the new law became clearly identified. A mixing of the old and the new had taken place, spurred by the Liberal Tories' advocacy of Christian political economy. Their parliamentary power had been considerable since the 1790s, and their economic views diverged sharply from those of the High Tories.[8] Both they and their spirit were represented on the Commission.

Richard Whately, the long-time fellow of Oriel and a Noetic, was in the vanguard of the Liberal Tories' conception of Christian political economy. His actions on the Commission marked the final break between himself and Newman and the Tractarians. Whately's *Introductory Lectures on Political Economy* was published in 1832, the year after he had left Oxford and the Drummond Chair of Political Economy to become archbishop of Dublin. In the *Lectures* Whately argued that his main objective was "to remove the impression existing in the minds of many, both of the friends and the adversaries of Christianity, as to the hostility between that and the conclusions of Political-Economy."[9] As far as the Tractarians were concerned, Whately was wasting his time. In their minds the gap could not be closed, since political economy was by definition irreligious and any attempt to harmonize it with Christianity was both impossible and heretical.

Despite Whately's protestations to the contrary, political economy was, as far as the Tractarians were concerned, an expression of detestable utilitarianism. They simply saw his association with the political economists as evidence of apostasy. Since the Tractarians insisted upon "a supernatural reference in politics and economics," observes William Peck, they could not accept Whately's stance.[10] To Newman, his former Oriel mentor had become "especially associated"[11] with liberal causes such as political economy. In so doing, Whately "made himself dead to me," Newman recalled later.[12]

The issue that undergirded the Whately-Newman rancor over political economy was the former's rejection of the exalted station accorded the Church by the Tractarians. The Church, Whately argued, was of human construction and was derived from faith, not generative of it. Faith was a function of "the inward motives and dispositions of the heart," he believed.[13] The Tractarians' glorification of the Church and denunciation of the state for alleged meddling was evidence of, in Whately's view, their abdication of reason. And he decried the Tractarians' replacement of reasoned faith with a misplaced apotheosis of the Church.

Similarly, Whately could see no sense in the Tractarians' objection to political economy and the state's role in the "*advancement* of civilization," as he put it.[14] Their view, in the words of Richard Soloway, that "a primitive Church undominated by rank or station and devoted to the labouring poor"[15] could respond well to the manifest afflictions of industrial Britain was mistaken. For Whately, the New Poor Law was a reasoned response to the needs of the country's poor and dispossessed, a recognition of the state's responsibility to the whole of society and the Church's inability alone to carry the load.

But to Newman and the Tractarians the Church was indeed all that was needed to direct society properly. The poor, Newman believed firmly, would be a fact of human society always and in that way should not be the object of elaborate plans of social engineering—which were bound to fail in any case—but rather should remain the necessary recipients of personal compassion and benevolence.[16] A reinvigorated Church would be the source of these social goods. The Church's chief function was to facilitate spiritual regeneration and to nurture the religious life. Thus the Tractarians' first principle of ministry to the poor was to minister to their souls. Social work, as a later generation would call it, was intensely personal to the Tractarians and carried with it a custodial responsibility lacking in secular, statist reform. The betterment of society required first the moral improvement of the individual. Accordingly, Newman consistently opposed "assigning political or civil motives for social and personal duties, and thereby withdrawing matters of conduct from the jurisdiction of religion," as Terence Kenny observes.[17]

The New Poor Law threw into sharp relief the contrasting positions of the Tractarians and political economists—both Christian and utilitarian. For Newman and his colleagues, the poor were blessed of God and in them He was working out his plan. Therefore, to legislate a method by which the poor might have their economic condition in life improved was to interfere with the divine order. It mattered little to the Tractarians that the New Poor Law did in fact embody the Christian idea that poverty was a means to bring out the best in people. To them, only the Church could mold such suffering in a way that was beneficial spiritually to the sufferer. The state's aims were categorically different from the Church's, believed the Tractarians, and had resulted in a mechanical charity epitomized by the "heartlessness"[18] of the workhouse, the cornerstone of the 1834 law, and a lessening of the impulse for private charity. As the Tractarian supporter S. R. Bosanquet wrote in the *British Critic:* "The true and requisite principle is, that private charity should outstrip the public provision; being so abundant and sufficient as to render the law unnecessary."[19] But if the Tractarians could find nothing to approve of in the state's attempt to deal with the industrial poor, then the inevitable question is what did they have to offer in its place that would both actualize their intense devotion to moral regeneration and individual goodwill and help the poor rise above their own material degradation?

For Newman, who late in life remarked not entirely truthfully that he had "never considered social questions in their relation to faith,"[20] the challenges posed by industrial Britain and its rapidly growing population did not greatly vex him. The British in aggregate did not enter his thinking. Newman was concerned with redeeming the souls of individuals. And certainly he was not interested in transforming their worldly standing.[21] As John Rowlands observes, to Newman, "the salvation of souls was infinitely more important than making individuals decent. Political reforms alone could never save men's souls."[22] Keble and, to a slightly lesser extent, Froude held views similar to Newman's. Together, they conceived of the Church as having an essentially spiritual, indeed salvific, mission to society. The Church was thought of by turns as rural and pastoral (Keble) or catholic and romantically attached to the downtrodden (Froude). And so of the leading Tractarians it was only Pusey who offered a more modern and elaborate, although scarcely less spiritual, approach to meeting the social needs of the British people in the nineteenth century.

Pusey's interest in the poor stemmed from his own privileged background as the second son of an aristocratic family in Berkshire. His father, the Honorable Phillip Pusey, was an archconservative and a High Churchman. Naturally, he was also a paternalist, and falling under his purview were the estate workers and poor townsfolk, in whom he took a close interest.[23] Edward and his elder brother Phillip, who would one day become a Tory M.P., were keenly aware of their father's sense of responsibility toward the poor, and each of them demonstrated a similar paternalistic attachment to those at the bottom of the social order. As Edward expressed it to Phillip in 1845: "We have a sort of hereditary right to speak for the poor, since sympathy with distress was [one] of our father's characteristics. . . . Let it be, if it please God, the business of your life, in whatever way He may put into your hands to benefit the poor. . . . It will indeed give a meaning, and centre, and direction to the remainder of your active life; it will shed a peace and joy over it."[24]

For Edward himself, the father's example provided the basis for an asceticism that greatly intensified following the early death of his wife Maria in 1839. In his grief Pusey resorted to a stringent domestic routine in which all luxury was done away with in order to more closely identify with the privations of the poor. As we know, by then he had already gone some way down this path by donating a very considerable sum to Bishop Charles Blomfield's church-building plan for the slums of London.[25]

Folding well into Pusey's attempt to identify more fully with the poor was his understanding of both the Oxford Movement as the expression of a "new Catholicism"[26] and the ancient Church's social mission. To Pusey, such a mission was predicated upon a profound understanding of the Eucharist as the means by which both to celebrate and to seal the idea of Christian communitarian oneness in the midst of a divisive society. He invested it with a social role not readily observable and, writes William Franklin, "held up the sacramental life as the noble heritage of the community of Christ."[27] Faith in Christ and adherence to the Church's ordained sacramental system would yield a new organic relationship between believers and the un-churched. Industrialization had created a society of intense alienation, person from person and class from class, he believed. The result, economically, opined Pusey, was that "the very clothes we wear are, while they are made, moistened by the tears of the poor."[28] Many of these tears, he believed, could be dried by the extension of genuine Christian fellowship grounded in eucharistic communitarianism.

Pusey's inherited paternalism, family circumstances, and expansive view of the social efficacy of the Eucharist were generative of his desire to reach out to the industrial poor, and these marks of his personality pushed him in various directions in an attempt to minister to the human detritus thrown up by the "dark, satanic mills" of Victorian Britain. Church-building in the slums of the industrial towns and cities was one area in which Pusey was involved heavily. As noted above, he was a keen supporter of Bishop Blomfield's work to this end in the great metropolis of London. Church-building elsewhere also was of great concern to Pusey, and his endowment of St. Saviour's, Leeds, stands as a monument to his munificence in this regard.[29] As well, he considered the creation of an Oxford-based college for the poor to gain training as clerks.[30] But it was Pusey's advocacy of the establishment of Anglican sisterhoods that is of special interest, given his interpretation of the Oxford Movement as evidence of a "new Catholicism" in Protestant England.

The Victorian Church of England witnessed the expansion of the role of women. The Church was "feminized" to a certain extent, and this move was true regardless of party affiliation: evangelical, Anglo-Catholic (Tractarian), or Broad.[31] For Pusey and the Anglo-Catholics, the Christian doctrine of womanhood included the foundationally conservative idea that woman had failed God first in the Garden of Eden and had then proceeded to lead man astray. The accepted literalness of the Genesis creation story undergirded this position, one the Anglo-Catholics shared with the evangelicals.

But while a basically conservative view of women that stressed subordination, domestic duties, and family nurturing was constant, such commonality between Anglo-Catholics and evangelicals ended with the former's belief in certain Roman practices. The Oxford Movement had revived the Catholic ideas of sisterhoods and priestly celibacy, the latter well demonstrated informally by Newman and Froude. The Anglo-Catholics also emphasized devotion to Mary, a position considerably less palatable to the Protestant population of England even than that of celibate priests. Indeed, Pusey's posthumous biographer, H. P. Liddon, was a prominent devotee of Mary and encouraged (Anglican) women to be governed by the example of Mary's "sweetness, her grace, her modesty, which so admirably adorn her rank."[32]

Pusey began to contemplate the establishment of Anglican women's orders in the late 1830s.[33] His favorite daughter, Lucy, early expressed a desire to live a celibate life in service to God, and her apparent devotion intensified Pusey's interest in Anglican sisterhoods. Like her mother before her in 1839, Lucy died young, in 1844, and a year later much in her honor the Sisters of Mercy came into existence in London. Pusey was the spiritual director of this community, known as Park Village because of its address. Soon other sisterhoods were established elsewhere in the country to engage in nursing, visitation, and education, especially among the poor.[34] General public criticism of their similarity to Roman Catholic women's orders predictably was swift in coming, but Pusey brushed it aside.[35]

Not so easily brushed aside, however, were objections from Anglican clergy in the dioceses affected, who found that the presence of the sisters caused considerable disquiet among many parishioners, as well as the wider populace.[36] The "Popish" bogeyman of course was behind these criticisms but that made them no less demanding of attention. For example, Bishop Blomfield found the criticism of the Park Village sisters so severe that he rejected any additional foundations in London and in 1855 wrote to Pusey "declin[ing] all further discussions of the [sisterhoods] question."[37] However, despite their unpopularity among much of the Anglican hierarchy the sisterhoods survived and even flourished.[38] Pusey stayed the course and remained their champion for the rest of his life.

Pusey did so within the context of what became perhaps the most important outlet for Anglican women seeking full-time work. By 1900, almost twenty years after Pusey's death, and fifty-five years after the founding of Park Village, over 10,000 women had joined over ninety sisterhoods. Some stayed briefly, others for a lifetime.

Motivations for joining a sisterhood varied: religious service; pity for the poor; inability to marry, or a disinclination for the institution itself; "career aspirations." Whatever the reason, Anglican sisterhoods offered some women a means to leave behind the prevailing assumptions about home and family that dominated Victorian society.[39]

As important as the sisterhoods were in the Oxford Movement's corporate impact on Anglican women in the nineteenth century, certain individual women need also be pointed out for their involvement with the Movement. Two prominent examples of "Tractarian lay women" are the poet Christina Rossetti and the novelist Charlotte Yonge.

As a child, Christina Rossetti was exposed to the teachings of the Oxford Movement through William Dodsworth, the Tractarian rector of Christ Church, Albany Street in London.[40] And the impression made on her there by the Movement was profound. As one of her biographers observes correctly: "This form of religion came to be, quite simply and without question, the most important thing in her life."[41] A few years after Rossetti and her family began to attend Christ Church she suffered a nervous breakdown. In 1845, while preparing for her Anglican confirmation, Rossetti's condition, to quote her understated brother William, "became obviously delicate."[42] She was not quite fifteen years old when the breakdown occurred, and it seems to have resulted from the spiritual and psychological strain brought on by the Tractarian demands for purity and holiness in advance of confirmation.[43] She remained ill until at least 1847 and emerged from this period with a changed mental character and compromised physical health. Her natural youthful exuberance had been quelled by the stringent demands of the Tractarians for reverence and reserve, and she now carried with her, to quote William again, "an awful sense of unworthiness, shadowed by an awful certainty [the reality of hell]."[44] As Jan Marsh notes, "the worthlessness of earth and the blessedness of heaven," pan-Christian themes to be sure but especially of Tractarianism, suffused Rossetti's mature poetry.[45]

Christina Rossetti's sustained spiritual encounter with the Oxford Movement yielded a body of poetry that made her one of the most celebrated of Victorian poets and a much-studied figure for later generations. But this encounter altered severely her personality—a thing not unexpected nor undesired in the demanding world of the Tractarians—and set up a considerable tension between her acquired religion and her natural temperament.

Charlotte Yonge, age thirty-five. Yonge's endorsement of the religious principles of the Oxford Movement was a feature of her many novels, the most famous of which was The Daisy Chain *(1856). By permission of The National Portrait Gallery, London.*

Rossetti's experience of Tractarianism intersects importantly with that of Charlotte Yonge's. As a young woman Rossetti read the latter's fiction and, to a degree, aspired to be like the heroines she found in it. "Miss Yonge," as she was (and is) known routinely, had an even closer identification with the Oxford Movement than Rossetti did. As a girl

Christina Rossetti *by her brother Dante Gabriel Rossetti. Rossetti's contemplative life and melancholy poetry were influenced deeply by the spirituality of the Oxford Movement. Ashmolean Museum, Oxford.*

Yonge had lived in John Keble's Hursley parish, and he prepared her for confirmation. She imbibed much "original Tractarianism"[46] from Keble, and her novels, once she had started down the still somewhat disreputable path of novel-writing, were written to convey some aspect of Tractarian truth. The remarkable thing about Yonge's writing is that it became popular despite its somewhat heavy-handed emphasis on morality and virtue. Someone who "saw her prime function always as a witness for the church"[47] is an unlikely person to have become one of the most popular novelists in Victorian Britain. But many of Yonge's carefully crafted novels were bestsellers, and she had wide appeal: from the unlikely precinct of officers serving in the Crimean War to the expected demographic of vicars' daughters. Her main audience consisted of upper-class and upper-middle-class young women who were given fictional models of ideal Christian women whose first duty was to God and the Church.[48] The attraction Yonge's writing and her spiritual essence held for Christina Rossetti is obvious.

Yonge's novels, such as *The Heir of Redclyffe* (1853) and *The Daisy Chain* (1856), achieved popularity because she made her characters interesting, sympathetic, and virtuous without making them priggish or propagandistic. Her self-proclaimed mission was to be "a sort of instrument for popularizing Church views."[49] And in this difficult task she achieved success. More to the point, she became the focus for a wider contemporary understanding of Tractarianism itself.

Both Rossetti and Yonge were dutiful Christian women in the manner expected by respectable Victorian society. Yonge was an overt exponent of the teachings of the Oxford Movement, whereas Rossetti remained much more reserved and introspective. Together, however, they form a tandem which did much then—and does much now—to illuminate the Oxford Movement's impact on Victorian (female) society and its proper apprehension by laypeople. As two such laypersons themselves, Rossetti and Yonge assumed the task of representing or, more clearly in Yonge's case, "popularizing" certain of the Movement's features. In so doing these two women helped greatly to diffuse the Oxford Movement's social ideas around the country.

The growth of lay Tractarianism and the wider dissemination of Church principles were also taken up through a variety of institutional means ranging from elementary education to poor relief. The management committees of bodies such as the National Society and the Additional Curates Society (ACS) often contained the same people.[50] The ACS, established in 1837 by a group of Anglican laymen concerned with rapid urban growth and the unchurched population was one of the most important social outlets for the Tractarians. The impetus for the creation of the ACS was the previous year's founding of an evangelical body, the Church Pastoral Aid Society (CPAS), designed to expand the number of curates assigned to parish churches and, controversially for High Churchmen and Tractarians, to employ "lay agents" in the performance of clerical duties. At first, in 1836, the CPAS hoped to do its work without causing strife within the Church. Alas, strife ensued. "The P.A. Society is very obstinate and self-willed,"[51] wrote Pusey to Newman in January 1837. Within a month William Gladstone, the strong Tractarian supporter and future prime minister, pulled out of the CPAS and joined in discussions for a separate society. In July, the result of these discussions, the ACS, was launched.

The ACS owed its founding primarily to Joshua Watson, the "benefactor of all his brethren," remembered Newman.[52] He was its guiding spirit and framed its constitution. A High Churchman of the old school, Watson had made a fortune during the Napoleonic wars but by 1814 had grown tired of the demands and compromises of business and turned his attention to seeking new and different ways of serving the Church. His range of involvements was wide and included the Society for the Propagation of the Gospel and, as we saw in Chapter 2, the *British Critic*. As a "Z" in the shorthand of the Tractarians, Watson could not support them without reservation. But his strong catholicity meant that he shared with them certain essentials regarding the Church and thus believed in the basic thrust of what they were attempting to do.

On the controversial issue of lay agency, they were of one mind. The provision of additional clergy for the great industrial towns and cities, not laymen, must be the focus of the ACS. "The 'Clergy Aid Society' is coming out under good auspices and on good principles,"[53] noted Pusey approvingly. Laymen were indispensable in the founding of the ACS but there was no question of their tampering with the Church's sacred orders. Priests must fulfill their ordained mandate; they must live up to their exalted position. High Churchmen and Tractarians both could endorse the stance taken by the ACS in this matter. A division over another issue would come soon enough of course, but in 1837 the ACS was a welcome vehicle for the spreading of Church principles.

"Populous places,"[54] as the constitution of the ACS termed the towns, comprised the focus for this dissemination, and the new society began its operations from a solid base. Its first subscription list contained some 650 names, many of them from the cream of society and many who were quite willing to contribute large sums of money in support of the goals of the ACS. King William IV, his life and reign about to end in 1837, donated three hundred pounds, for example.[55] Victoria, the new sovereign, added her name to the list immediately. And so it went. Lay and clerical support, both high and low in station, characterized the membership list of the ACS.

High Churchmen and Tractarians continued to cooperate closely in the ACS for the first few years of its existence. Pusey, Keble, and Newman all contributed financially to the ACS, as did a number of Tractarian supporters.[56] Pusey, especially, was gratified by how the ACS devoted itself to the traditional conception of priestly service while at the same time extending its reach into urban England with the express help of laypeople. "It is very pleasing to see how completely J[oshua] W[atson] identifies himself with us,"[57] wrote Pusey to Keble in the autumn of 1839. And as Pusey told Watson himself: "How cheering to be recognized by you as carrying on the same torch wh[ich] we had received from yourself, and those of your generation, who had remained faithful to the old teaching."[58]

Such mutual admiration began to weaken, however, with the cumulative effects of Froude's anti-Protestant *Remains,* the conflict over the Martyrs' Memorial, and the publication of *Tract 90.* Watson and the other High Churchmen, never as "completely" in agreement with the Tractarians as Pusey supposed, began to pull back from the Catholic extremism that was beginning to mark the Oxford Movement by around 1840. For Watson and the inner council of the ACS, Gladstone's brand of Tractarianism, based on an unbending devotion to the Church of England, had been the most recognizable face of the Movement. Thus it came as a shock when the Oxford-based Tractarians—notably New-man—began to display an apparent sympathy for the Church of Rome. Such an attraction was completely unacceptable to the staunchly Protestant Watson. But Watson valued highly the Tractarians' recalling to the Church certain of its essential principles, and thus he refused to join the chorus condemning the Tractarians, now growing around the country. He discussed the situation at length with Edward Churton, a fellow High Churchman and his eventual biographer, and Churton concurred with his friend over the Tractarians: "But as things are, it is impossible for any man who so far agrees with them as I do, to take any overt act against them, without laying himself open to the suspicion of wishing to save himself at their expence [*sic*], and to abandon them in a time of persecution, when he has had the benefit of the influence of their writings and friendly co-operation before the strife began."[59]

And Churton and Watson maintained this view for some time, refusing to desert the Oxford men when criticism of them became fierce.[60] Nor did the Tractarians, save Newman, desert the ACS. In the wake of Newman's departure for Rome Keble and Pusey maintained their support of the society. Pusey, especially, found the ACS's guiding principle of urban outreach to lie at the heart of his own vision of the Church's social task. Watson, like the Tractarians too, denounced the 1834 Poor Law: "From the moment a Government calling itself Christian could deliberately pass such an act, I confess I am a radical, and have ceased to hope for any good as long as it remains."[61] The Church must act up to its historic mandate and reassert itself as the nation's almshouse. Watson's concern for the urban poor and dispossessed meant that the ACS routinely turned down requests for support from rural parishes.[62] He believed that the ACS was uniquely equipped to minister to the needs of urban populations. And in this view support was liable to come from the most unlikely of places. Much later, in 1861, Benjamin Disraeli, Anglican convert and reformed dandy, and later in the decade briefly Conservative prime minister, addressed the ACS. "The Church has never found the great towns," he said. "They are her future; and it will be in the great towns that the greatest triumphs of the Church will be achieved; for the greater the population, and the greater the task, the greater the triumph."[63] Even today, the ACS continues to operate with urban outreach as its focus.

The ACS is a useful reference point in probing the Oxford Movement's social impact on Victorian Britain. As an organization in which laypeople were prominent, the ACS reveals the extent to which Tractarianism shared in the renewed sense of social responsibility that characterized the whole Church of England—parties and people, clerical and lay—in the nineteenth century. Tractarianism's Oxford base has made it natural for historians and others to concentrate their efforts on events there to the partial exclusion of those in other parts of the country.[64] But the Oxford Movement's wider impact demands a wider examination, as we have seen demonstrated partially in the ACS. Another area in which we can witness the Movement's broader impact is in architecture and the Anglican Gothic Revival of the 1830s and 1840s.

In 1834, erstwhile Anglican Augustus Welby Northmore Pugin (1812–52) converted to Roman Catholicism. For British church architecture there has probably never been a more important conversion. Pugin's adoption of his new faith was complete and, like most new converts, full of ardor, and it manifested itself in the championing of the "Pointed Architecture" (i.e. Gothic) of Roman Catholic churches of the Middle Ages. Such architecture with its high altars, groined ceilings, vaulted piers, buttresses, and stone, argued Pugin in *Contrasts* (1836 and 1841),[65] embodied the true expression of the Christian faith, which in England had been destroyed wantonly by the Protestant Reformation and the loathsome Henry VIII. Pugin believed that in England the proper physical expression of Christianity could not be achieved unless Gothic church architecture was revived.

Pugin's polemic was not issued in an architectural vacuum, however; his was not a lone voice crying in the wilderness. The romantics, such as William Wordsworth and Samuel Taylor Coleridge, had helped to prepare the way with their devotion to medieval myth and religion, which in their view, had marked the pastoral England of preindustrial and pre-Protestant times. Thomas Rickman and Matthew Bloxam had advocated recovering one aspect of this vanished world, the Gothic style in architecture, in books published in 1817 and 1829.[66] A certain fashionable acceptance had been confirmed already in 1807 at London's Carlton House and then again in 1824 at Windsor Castle when royalty gave the style its blessing. Then when Parliament and the Palace of Westminster were destroyed by fire in 1834, Gothic was stipulated as one of the styles in which they should be rebuilt. Indeed, by the time construction began in 1840 Pugin had been contracted to design much of the detail of the massive structure. Pugin's appointment to work on Westminster symbolizes the central role his writings and his design played in the Gothic Revival that came to embody early-mid Victorian ecclesiology. One of the most important results of this trend was to put into brick and stone the ideals of the Oxford Movement.

Pugin's impassioned advocacy of the Gothic style quickly found a favorable response among many Anglicans, especially those whose sympathies lay with the High Church party and the Tractarians. George Gilbert Scott (1811–78) is perhaps the most notable Anglican architect of the period whose imagination was quickened by Pugin and whose own architectural designs did much to enlarge and ensure the outward face of the Anglican revival. The evangelicals, with their horror of anything that suggested Rome, thought the Church of England should avoid what they considered Catholic excesses, but the forces behind the Gothic Revival were much stronger than those mustered by the evangelicals, whose public influence was now on the wane.

At the universities of Oxford and Cambridge architectural societies were formed that were animated greatly by the Gothic gospel preached by Pugin and Scott, as well as (later) by William Butterfield (1814–1900). The journal, *The Ecclesiologist,* became a kind of handbook for the Gothic Revival. Spurred by the architectural demands of ecclesiologists and by the Tractarians' desire for deeper worship, more frequent celebrations of the Eucharist, an exalted understanding of the Church, and a higher view of the clergy, many Anglican churches began to display the full Gothic panoply: carved pinnacles, tiled roofs, stained-glass windows, detailed metalwork, and for the clergy, vestments. Indeed, anything that bespoke the richness of medieval worship came to characterize the Gothic Revival in its mid-century apotheosis.

As we have seen earlier, church-building was a central preoccupation of many Anglicans as the industrial revolution transformed the English land- and cityscape in the nineteenth century. The Gothic Revival provided an additional impetus to this trend, an ecclesiological imperative. The speed and frequency with which churches were built is astonishing. From 1830 to 1861 some fifteen hundred Anglican churches were erected in England. Over the second half of the century approximately one hundred churches were built each year and almost every existing Anglican church was restored in some way.[67] Later, the Gothic Revival diffused into a search for a theoretical Ideal,[68] but in the early stages of the movement, the ideal, which did lend itself to varied interpretations, was the Catholic cathedral of the High Middle Ages. The Gothic Revival changed the physical expression of Victorian Anglicanism while at the same time the Oxford Movement altered its orthopraxis. Together, they succeeded in expressing a deeper historical sense of the Church of England and in the process altered both the physical and the spiritual apprehension of Anglicanism.

The Tractarians and the ecclesiologists envisaged an organic society based on the religious verities provided by a renewed Church of England. But this expectation, however firmly held, had to take into account the ironic fact that despite the robust church-building activity of the second half of the nineteenth century the British population was steadily becoming less overtly religious.[69] Meanwhile politically, the Church of England, as we have seen, had had to give ground to Dissent and to Roman Catholics in particular. While the establishment was not about to give way completely, Anglican privilege had been significantly reduced. And probably no one in the religio-political world felt this diminution more keenly than the lay Tractarian William Ewart Gladstone. Yet, in time, he also came to represent perhaps better than anyone else the slow emergence of liberalism in Victorian religion and politics. How and why did this transformation take place? And how do we account, as well, for the conservative Oxford Movement's gradual accommodation of liberalism later in the nineteenth century?

William Gladstone was always the "biggest beast in the forest," as his most recent biographer calls him.[70] Religion and politics were at the center of his life, and in this joint realm he strode, never unopposed, but seldom defeated. A wealthy father and an Eton and Oxford education prepared Gladstone for life in the "forest" of Victorian religion and politics, a place he remained from his first election to the House of Commons in 1832 until his final retirement in 1896, a Herculean sixty-four years.

Gladstone's childhood was spent imbibing the sturdy precepts of evangelicalism at the knee of his devout mother. But as a young man he migrated to High Church Anglicanism from which he observed keenly the writings and actions of the Tractarians. By the time the Oxford Movement got under way in the summer of 1833 Gladstone had graduated from the university, decided against taking holy orders, and was embarking on a parliamentary career. But religious questions consumed him always, and he studied closely the position of the Church in the British political establishment. He heartily endorsed the revivification of the Church initially called for by the Oxford men. While Gladstone's exact relationship to the Tractarians is a point of debate,[71] there is no doubt that he found both their early ecclesiastical politics and their on-going spiritual discipline highly attractive. On the latter point he never wavered. In old age he wrote to a friend in defense of Tractarianism: "If the business of Christianity be the formation of Christ in the souls of men, it was surely progressive, and England at this day bears witness among many opposite signs, to its progressiveness."[72]

Gladstone's religious journey, one which could see him lauding the Tractarians in his eighties, was always intense and sometimes mystifying. "Gladstone," notes E. J. Feuchtwanger, "was always in need of causes to which he could fully commit himself."[73] During the 1830s, the chosen cause was the revival of the Church of England. To this end Gladstone thought hard and wrote extensively, publishing two books detailing his considered interpretation of what constituted the proper relationship between church and state. The state, wrote Gladstone in *The State in Its Relations with the Church* (1838), was an "organic body" where individuals were "constituents of the active power of that life. . . . The state is the self-governing energy of the nation made objective."[74] The state had a conscience, Gladstone believed in accordance with his Aristotelianism, one that required tutoring by the church. Indeed, the "highest duty" of the state was to maintain "close relations of cooperation" with the church.[75]

In Gladstone's second treatise, *Church Principles Considered in*

Their Results (1840), he elaborated more fully his idea of the organic state and the tutoring church. Of the latter, Gladstone claimed that it was responsible "for the social condition at large"[76] and needed the state's benevolence to perform this function. A unified society provided the best hope for just governance and social regeneration, and in this view Gladstone found general agreement with the Tractarians.[77] But in the late 1830s and early 1840s this was not a very realistic ideal.

While writing *The State in Its Relations with the Church* and *Church Principles Considered in Their Results,* Gladstone was keenly aware of the challenges to his ideal posed by the gradual liberalizing of the British polity seen most clearly since the era of intense reform spanning the years from 1828 to 1832. Yet he held stubbornly onto the organic ideal and indeed was never to surrender it completely.[78] But by the 1840s Gladstone had to face the reality that the confessional state belonged to another age and that "should England nationally repudiate the Catholic Church, it is not, I apprehend, by parliamentary evangelisation that she can be recalled to a sense of her duty because what is done in Parliament must be evolution of its own recognized laws & constitutive ideas."[79]

Gladstone shared with his Tractarian friends the pessimism that devotion to the organic ideal was unlikely to be rewarded in their unsympathetic age. Gladstone was "reluctantly convinced," as he wrote to Newman in 1844, "that from year to year the capacity of the State to sustain a religious character diminishes."[80] Gladstone was vexed greatly by the problem of reconciling Anglican privilege with the rights of the Dissenter, and to effect this reconciliation, he ultimately made peace with the political reality of religious pluralism, as David Bebbington points out.[81] Such a concession of course was beyond Newman's comprehension at the time and scarcely less acceptable to Keble and Pusey. Keble had reviewed Gladstone's *State and Church* in the *British Critic*[82] in 1839, and in the main he disapproved of what he found in it. Gladstone's career as a politician compromised his essential churchmanship, Keble believed. Gladstone, he lamented, "survey[s] with too favourable an eye the alliance as it exists."[83] Keble regretted Gladstone's continued hope that the state might be cleansed of its sin of violating the Church's spiritual integrity. The state was beyond reclamation in Keble's eyes, and the paramount issue was saving the Church's freedom from the Erastian hand of Westminster. As Perry Butler describes it: "There was nothing more to be dreaded than that the Church, for fear of losing popularity or courting hostility, should in any way forgo her sacred principles for the sake of retaining her connection with the State."[84]

For Gladstone, the rejection of the state by the Tractarians was a heavy blow, to be sure. But there was no chance that he would follow them in their extreme course. Despite their altered alliance, church and state constituted a necessary, though flawed, unity in Gladstone's mind that must in some manner be retained. He was in politics to serve the Church, as he maintained, and only through the continuation of the establishment could he live out his own purpose and the nation itself be best governed. Gladstone's sympathies in spiritual matters were always with the Tractarians, and through the Additional Curates Society and "The Engagement," a lay Tractarian brotherhood whose formation was suggested by Keble and to which Gladstone belonged,[85] he contributed actively to the cause of Church renewal. But he could never abandon the establishment for in it lay his life's calling and work as a Christian politician.

The Tractarians, on the other hand, had a varied view of the establishment ranging from Froude's denunciation of it, to Newman's departure from it, to Keble and Pusey's ambivalence about it. Gladstone's intellectual accommodation of the pluralist state gave him a way to move from conservatism to liberalism. He never relinquished his belief in the necessity of elites, however. As he remarked to an unreceptive John Ruskin in 1878, "I am a firm believer in the aristocratic principle—the rule of the best. I am an out-and-out *inequalitarian.*"[86] Yet Gladstone did modify radically his apprehension of ordinary people and their latent interest in and potential stewardship of political and social reforms. He lost his conservative fear of the masses and came to see in them a demonstrated desire for freedom, prosperity, and peace. Late in life he summed up his own transformation this way: "I was brought up to distrust and dislike liberty; I learned to believe in it."[87]

Gladstonian liberalism was a unique strain of the great nineteenth-century school of thought owing very little to that on display in France and elsewhere on the Continent—the antitraditional, utilitarian, and secular kind of liberalism that was the great enemy according to the

Tractarians. Still, the fact that their successor Anglo-Catholics were able to come to terms with Gladstonian liberalism later in the century is remarkable. From their point of origin denouncing Whig-liberal depredations of the Church to their place of accommodating themselves to high Victorian liberalism, the intellectual journey of the Tractarians/ Anglo-Catholics is important in understanding their later impact on British society. Much of the reason for this accommodation lies in the nature of Gladstonian liberalism itself.

The Liberal Party under Gladstone was not a political party in the modern sense but rather a movement of different ideas, people, religions, and classes that came together in a working coalition under his inspired leadership. The centrality of Gladstone himself to the workings of the party and to its fortunes was seen clearly in its splintering and demise in the years that followed his resignation of the leadership in 1894. But while he remained its chief the party prospered and thus was able to encompass a number of contradictions. For our purposes, the contradiction of greatest interest was that of the Anglo-Catholics' presence in Liberal ranks of any sort, Gladstonian or otherwise.

Church and chapel begetting conservative and liberal is the usual construction historians place upon the religio-political landscape of Victorian Britain. And this construction is correct, in the main. As Gladstone admitted readily in 1877, chapelgoers comprised "the backbone of British Liberalism."[88] Naturally, of course, there were many others whose political allegiance lay with Gladstone and among this number were counted Anglo-Catholics. Gladstone's own high churchmanship found expression in some Anglo-Catholic practices; and though he never became a ritualist in practice, he did not shy away from championing the ritualist cause when it met crisis in 1874.

The Public Worship Regulation Bill brought before Parliament by the Conservatives in that year was one of the main means by which Disraeli sought to cement to the Conservative Party the political support of the majority Protestant population of the Church of England. "Catholic practices" were becoming too blatant for some Anglicans to accept, and the Conservatives aimed to satisfy the complaint by intervening in the life of the Church. Gladstone was outraged at this latest example of the ongoing Erastian menace and quickly became the parliamentary champion of the ritualists. The fact that he could also go to battle against the detested Disraeli doubtless added a certain *frisson* to the impending clash.

The ritualist crisis did much to convince the Anglo-Catholics that in Gladstone they had a champion of Church principles. As noted earlier, Gladstone had never abandoned his belief in the organic ideal. Though forced to accommodate a degree of pluralism politically, he always decried the state's interference in the affairs of the Church. Forcing a change in the style of worship itself was anathema to Gladstone and in defense of the prerogatives of the Church he treated the House of Commons to a protracted volley of righteous criticism directed at the government benches. His intervention late in the debate, which ran through the spring and summer of 1874, was "like a thunder clap"[89] wrote Disraeli's main biographer Robert Blake. Gladstone ridiculed the Conservatives, who intended, he said, to pass "a Bill to put down Ritualism."[90] With his majority government, Disraeli won the day eventually and the bill passed. But henceforth he was seen as a "sworn foe" by Anglo-Catholics, who would see some of their clergy prosecuted under the provisions of the Act.[91]

For the remainder of Gladstone's politically active life he was the favored politician of Anglo-Catholics, and they accepted his and the Liberal Party's brand of liberalism because in Gladstone's hands it had come to represent freedom, especially the freedom to pursue the religious practices of choice. The heirs of the Oxford Movement were able to accommodate this exceptional liberalism mainly because it was filtered through the trusted lens of Gladstone. As "the chief facet of the prism through which the light of late-Victorian Liberalism gained coherence,"[92] observes Colin Matthew, Gladstone was a believable and sound presence in politics for Anglo-Catholics. His high view of the Church reassured Anglo-Catholics as to his essential trustworthiness, and in episodes such as the ritualist controversy Gladstone proved to them his religious fidelity.

As was suggested in our treatment of the 1834 Poor Law, the Tractarians—and their heirs—objected strongly to the expanding role of the state in social affairs. Both they and Gladstone were convinced of the necessity of individual agency in determining one's lot in life. As the architect of the "minimal state" during his years as chancellor of the exchequer and then prime minister, Gladstone believed firmly that it was the responsibility of individuals, voluntary agencies, and the Church to meet the social requirements of the people. Expanding the state to do so would mean sapping self-reliance and the loss of the moral and spiritual rewards contingent upon personal reclamation. This strain of conservative social thinking in Gladstone appealed greatly to the Anglo-Catholics, and his obvious sympathy for their churchmanship reassured them. Thus for most of the remainder of the century Gladstonian liberalism was an acceptable political creed for Anglo-Catholics to hold.

The Tractarians and Anglo-Catholics occupy an important place in the history of Victorian society. Their religious beliefs shaped closely their apprehension of the reasons for social inequities and what might be done to ease the lot of those at the bottom of the social order. The belief that the Church could and should minister to the poor and dispossessed was their answer and thus remained central to their own social project and important to the Church of England at large. This belief manifested itself most visibly in a recovery of the Gothic architectural form, which spoke clearly of the organic society the Tractarians idealized, a society in which the Church occupied the lead role in caring for the poor. It also manifested itself in the establishment of women's orders and in the initiative of laypeople to create organizations—such as the Additional Curates Society—designed to enlarge the Church's reach in industrial Britain.

The Oxford Movement's impact on Victorian social affairs, however, was circumscribed both by its leaders' own reluctance to concern themselves greatly with temporal concerns (Pusey excepted), and by a society whose loudest voices in the field were those belonging to statists. The result was an uneven impact and the assumption by succeeding generations that the Tractarians had nothing to say, or nothing of consequence to say, on the subject of the poor, or women, or on social questions generally. But as has been suggested in this chapter, where the Oxford Movement's leaders and its heirs chose to engage Victorian society, the encounter usually demonstrated the existence of a clear position, consonant with Church principles, and dedicated to the spiritual integrity of the individual.

5 Missions

The Oxford Movement's call for a reassertion of catholic principles within the Church of England was by its essential nature missiological. They had a story of Church renewal to tell, and they and their supporters were keen to tell it, whenever and wherever they could. The nineteenth century, of course, was the great age of British missionary endeavor, and the Oxford Movement's participation in this zealous modern Christian crusade came naturally, although not unreservedly, as we shall see. As John Davies observes, there was about the Movement a kind of "consecrated aggressiveness."[1] Tractarian influence was felt wherever the Church of England existed throughout the world during the mid-Victorian period. The British Empire gave the Church of England an obvious advantage in spreading the faith, governance, and culture of orthodox Christianity. But the prominence and zest of other denominations and missionary bodies made for a multifarious religious presence in most places where the Union Jack flew. This fact was as true in an old settler colony such as Canada as it was in a much less valued and much less developed corner of the empire such as Central Africa.

The standardbearers of Tractarianism found out quickly, too, that the party cleavages of the Church of England at home were seen readily abroad. The Catholic-Protestant animosity that so marked the relation-

ship between the domestic Oxford Movement and its opponents did not
weaken when exported to the far-flung reaches of the empire, as well as
to the anglophilic culture found in the United States. This chapter is
concerned largely with probing how the Oxford Movement was part of
the larger British missionary thrust of the middle years of the nineteenth
century and where and how its ideas were disseminated and received, or
not received. My intention, therefore, is not to provide a history of the
colonial church, but rather to point out the major instances of the Oxford Movement's impact within the British Empire and the United
States in order to better understand the Movement's sense of mission
abroad.

As the most significant era of Western missionary expansion, the
long nineteenth century, from 1789 to 1914, spawned countless societies
devoted to Christian proselytizing. The English Baptists led the way by
forming a missionary society in 1792, and within a decade they had
been joined by a number of others, including the London Missionary
Society—mostly Congregationalist—and the Anglican Church Missionary Society (CMS). Scarcely had another decade passed before all the
major European countries as well as the United States harbored missionary societies of one sort or another. The growth continued unabated,
and as one of the leading historians of missions, the late Stephen Neill
notes, "by the end of the century every nominally Christian country and
almost every denomination had begun to take its share in the support of
the missionary cause."[2]

Given conventional mission work's evangelistic core the CMS was
predominantly evangelical in temperament and composition. High and
latitudinarian Anglicans, on the other hand, had long supported the
Society for Promoting Christian Knowledge (SPCK), which had been in
existence since the beginning of the eighteenth century and which had
made some efforts in overseas missionary work even though its focus lay
mainly in domestic outreach. Like the SPCK, the first major field of
operations for the CMS was India, the vast and, to contemporaries, be-
wildering subcontinent that the British were gradually putting under
their suzerainty from the mid-eighteenth to the mid-nineteenth centuries. The East India Company spearheaded this project, and its position
was solidified in Bengal in 1757 upon Robert Clive's victory at the Battle

of Plassey. After that, the Company made steady progress both commer-
cially and politically. During this period, in 1806, Henry Martyn of the
CMS arrived in Calcutta fresh from Cambridge, at that time favored by
evangelicals over Oxford. Martyn was a brilliant scholar and linguist and
succeeded quickly in translating the New Testament into Urdu. Martyn
died young, however, at age thirty-one in 1812, but his selfless service
and high intellectual tone cast a long shadow over Anglican missionary
work in India and elsewhere.[3]

Expansion by the CMS in India, and after 1829 by the Society for
the Propagation of the Gospel in Foreign Parts (SPG)—formed to take
over the SPCK's limited foreign missionary work—was seen in many
other places as well. The Church of England had a deep history in the
United States, of course; and the British colonies to the north, most of
which would unite to form the Dominion of Canada in 1867, were likewise steeped (French-speaking Quebec excepted) in the dominant religious tradition of the mother country.[4] The same can be said for the
nascent Australian colonies. South Africa, too, developed a strong Anglican presence emanating from Cape Town. Indeed, wherever the sun
shone on the British Empire in the nineteenth century, it shone on
parishes and missions of the Church of England as well. The CMS and
the SPG, despite their ecclesiological differences, worked mostly in harmony in an effort to ensure that Britain's robust imperial project was
fortified by an attendant establishment Christianity.[5]

The pervasiveness of the consciousness of empire in British society
meant that the cultural importance of missionary work increased
throughout the nineteenth century.[6] It reached its apogee in the 1860s
and 1870s through the demonstrated heroism of David Livingstone, the
great Scots medical missionary sent out originally to southern Africa in
1840 by the London Missionary Society (LMS). By the time the celebrated doctor-explorer died in south-central Africa in 1873 and was bur-
ied the next year at Westminster Abbey in one of the great set-piece
spectacles of the Victorian age, he had come to embody the national
mission of the British nation: civilization, Christianity, and commerce.
Britain was to be a light to the rest of the world and in the process
"uplift" the "lesser" races in order that they might be "redeemed" and
"improved." Such rhetoric strikes hard against ears conditioned by

twenty-first-century sensibilities about race and cultural equality. But within Victorian society, alive to this kind of muscular Christianity, the aims of the civilizing mission were both worthy and achievable. And to the Church of England, the sometime "chaplain to Empire," these aims were especially important.

Both in the capitals of empire and in its outposts the Church of England was a physical presence representing God's (and Anglicanism's) work in the same way that Government House symbolized the political power of the faraway metropolis. Church and state were not necessarily and at all times each other's helpmeet, but when and where they did clash, the resultant wound was usually bound up in the sure knowledge that each needed the other to maintain the unity and integrity of Britain's mission, regardless of where on the globe it had touched down. This acceptable overseas Erastianism displayed a commitment to the establishment the nature of which was well demonstrated at home. Rule Britannia, indeed.

The Oxford Movement's own sense of mission fit well the imperatives of an age given over to exploration, redemption, and improvement. The Tractarians' consciousness of the territorial extent of the empire and the expansion of the Church overseas was limited initially, however. Their primary concern, as we know, was local and national. Not surprisingly, style of churchmanship was the issue which first placed overseas missions in the way of the Tractarians, and it came through Newman's encounter with the CMS. As a young Oriel fellow and Church of England ordinand Newman visited the London headquarters of the CMS in 1824 to see what was required in order to become one of their missionaries.[7] Though made with Newman's typical seriousness, this visit does not seem to have led to a consideration of going overseas because quickly thereafter he took up the curacy of St. Clement's in Oxford, which was in Oriel's gift.

Newman's relations with the CMS did not end with his brief reconnaissance of its workings in 1824, however. He maintained a strong interest in missions, and a few years later, in 1829, he was elected joint secretary of the Oxford branch of the CMS. And despite his increasing High Churchmanship by this time, he plunged into his duties on behalf of the predominantly evangelical body. Predictably, what he found there dismayed him, and before the end of the year he had filed an official protest with the CMS over the evangelical content of some of the sermons preached on its behalf.

Newman's protest was based on the evident evangelicalism of the Society as manifested in the preaching of its supporting clergy. He enlarged his protest by writing and publishing anonymously a pamphlet at the beginning of 1830 bearing the wordy title: "Suggestions respectfully offered to Resident Clergymen of the University, in behalf of the Church Missionary Society." In it, Newman argued that the Society and its preachers needed to be brought under closer control of the bishops whose duty it was to uphold professed Anglican doctrine against the depredations of an insidious evangelicalism.[8] Newman's protest was greeted coldly by Oxford's mostly evangelical membership, and he was not reelected secretary at the annual general meeting of the Society in March.[9]

Despite the rejection of his protest Newman's association with the CMS did not end entirely in 1830. He remained an ordinary member of the Society for four more years. But in his view the irredeemably evangelical nature of the Society made a closer association with it impossible. Newman was becoming more alive to the idea of the centrality of the Church and its principles regarding what constituted genuine Christian (missionary) activity: the use only of ordained Anglican clergy, the establishment of bishoprics, and so on. He saw, thereby, missionary work outside the established Church (he resigned from the British Bible Society in 1830) as necessarily deleterious to its strength. Instead of allowing a creeping evangelicalism to infect the CMS, the clergy should stand firm upon the doctrine of the Church. Why, Newman stated, should the Society provide another enemy when the Church "has already enemies enough."[10]

Only the year before, in 1829, as noted above, the SPG had been formed to more closely reflect the desires of High Churchmen for foreign missions based on Church principles. Newman, curiously, is silent on the SPG. This body eventually would reflect his conception of proper mission work. But in the last years before the Oxford Movement began, Newman's greatest interests and concerns took him elsewhere and the SPG caused no evident ripple in his mind.

Whatever Newman's deeper concern for missions may have been, the imbroglio with the CMS removed him from a close association with Anglican expansion abroad. For Keble, the parochial interests of Hursley remained most important and thus the workings of the Church within the empire did not have an appreciable impact on him. Froude, however, did experience firsthand the Church of England abroad and was the only one of the Tractarians to do so. As we noted in Chapter 3, Froude went to Barbados late in 1833 to find relief from the relentlessly debilitating effects of his tuberculosis.

Upon arriving at the Church of England's Codrington College in Barbados Froude took up the temporary position of chaplain to Bishop William Coleridge, a High Churchman of the "Z" school. His relations with the bishop were by turns cordial and rocky, with disagreement over the controversial issue of the emancipation of the slaves providing the centerpiece of their recurring animosity. Additionally, the two men clashed over the admissions policy of the college, which under Coleridge, had become an exclusive preserve of "gentlemen," that is to say, local men of social standing. But since that species was in short supply in colonial Barbados, the college was almost empty of students.[11] Froude was outraged by this elitist policy: "The notion that a priest must be a gentleman is a stupid exclusive protestant fantasy, and ought to be exploded. If they would educate a lower caste here, they would fill the college directly," he wrote to Newman.[12]

But the slavery issue annoyed Froude even more. The long campaign by the heavily evangelical abolitionists to outlaw the slave trade within the British Empire resulted in victory in 1833–34. Evangelical agitation had done much to bring about this victory, and its acknowledged leader, William Wilberforce, lived just long enough to witness the fruits of his efforts. But Froude hated the "cant" of philanthropy employed by the abolitionists and their strident evangelicalism. Patronizingly, he considered the slaves wholly unready for freedom and its attendant responsibilities and sadly representative of the despised abolitionists: "I am ashamed to say I cannot get over my prejudices against the niggers," Froude wrote in September 1834, "every one I meet seems to me like an incarnation of the whole Anti-slavery Society."[13] Moreover, he believed that the profitable plantations, the source of Caribbean prosperity, were headed for rack and ruin once their source of forced labor was withdrawn. Froude's view, of course, is racist and capitalist, but in its own time had great social and economic currency.

At the core of Froude's objection was a concern for the Church's ability to survive and prosper in the West Indies once the source of its upkeep—the planter class—had been crippled financially. Bishop Coleridge, on the other hand, advocated a gradual emancipation to which both master and slave could adjust. At any rate, Froude thought Coleridge and other genteel High Churchmen like him had made the Church in the West Indies slack. As for the local population, he despised them: "The thing that strikes me as most remarkable in the cut of these niggers is excessive immodesty; a forward, stupid familiarity, intended for civility, which prejudices me against them."[14] In Froude's mind, at least, the missionary experiment was a failure in the otherwise beautiful sugar islands of the Caribbean. But, given his vulgar view of the inhabitants of the region, a higher view of them was impossible to hold in any event. "The negro features are so horridly ugly," he wrote early in 1834, " at least the generality of them: now and then indeed one sees the finely chiselled Egyptian features, and among others one can distinctly trace the difference of caste in all shades from man to monkey."[15]

The offensiveness of this kind of language to modern ears need not be dwelt upon. Unfortunately, and more to the point, Froude did not provide for posterity a considered view of missionary endeavor, although it is clear that he agreed with Newman that Anglican missions should adhere to Church principles and not degrade themselves by associating with the evangelical Protestant missions, who in their view, displayed scant regard for sacramental, ordered Christianity.[16]

Froude returned from Barbados in 1835, not having grown fond of his temporary tropical home over the course of nearly two years. Earlier, however, in characteristic language he had begrudged the place a compliment concerning his own precarious health: "Niggerland is a poor substitute for the *limen apostolorum*. However, I do verily believe that if I had stayed in England I should have had a confirmed disease on my lungs by this time."[17] England fulfilled his expectation; Froude died the next year.

Froude's early death, Newman's falling-out with the CMS and

ultimate departure for the Roman Church, and Keble's quiet life in rural
England—circumstances and choice conspired to remove the founding
Tractarian troika from the Church of England or, in Keble's case, from
its mainstream of activity, including missions. Thus, "of all the Oxford
Tractarians," observes David Forrester rightly, "Pusey took Anglican
expansion overseas the most seriously."[18] Part of this interest was simply
a function of longevity: Pusey lived until 1882 and in so doing witnessed
the beginnings of the fin-de-siècle flowering of the Victorian missionary
imperative. But more important than the widespread popularity of
Christian missions was Pusey's deep interest in and commitment to the
expansion of the Church of England, both at home and abroad, providing such expansion could be accomplished on the basis of sound Church
principles.

Pusey's commitment to and understanding of missions was made
public initially in 1838 when he preached a pair of sermons in which he
enunciated his position on the proper method for Anglican expansion
overseas.[19] Pusey told the assembled parishioners of Melcombe Regis
that most of the large missionary societies had gotten it wrong with their
undisciplined, "desultory" manner of sending forth missionaries. Rather,
the "missionary society set forth in the Prophets, by our Lord and by
his Apostles, is, the Church." Without the Church at the center of the
enterprise, missions lacked "order" and a "regular ministerial system,"
he charged. Further, he said: "Church history is full of accounts of holy
men, who were sent forth as Bishops, and were Apostles of the nations
to whom they were sent, and founded Churches, and converted great
nations: but there is not one account of persons going out of their own
will, or establishing a Church without Bishops, or without having received a commission so to do from those who had inherited the power
to give it, the bishops of the Church."[20] Pusey concluded by commend-
ing the SPG's sound method of missionary deployment, calling the society "the accredited organ of the whole Episcopacy of our branch of the
Church Catholic . . . it has ever gladly submitted itself to our Bishops
abroad, and placed its missionaries at their disposal."[21]

Around this time Pusey corresponded regularly with Charles
Blomfield, bishop of London and supporter of the Colonial Bishoprics'

Fund, a body established to ensure the type of Church expansion endorsed by Pusey, and Archdeacon Benjamin Harrison, who possessed a keen interest in the missionary Church. Blomfield, an eminently practical churchman, was not entirely receptive to Pusey's insistence on complete Church independence in the naming of overseas bishops. Harrison, conversely, a Tractarian, endorsed heartily Pusey's stance.[22] This stance, worked out in the late 1830s and early 1840s, would remain Pusey's considered position for the rest of his life.[23] So, too, did it become the considered position taken by Anglo-Catholics on missions.

Public interest in missions was given a great push forward in the late 1850s upon David Livingstone's return to England from Africa. Not the least of those impressed by the selfless work and inspiring words of the resolute Scotsman were the Anglo-Catholic heirs of the Oxford Movement. The tenets of Tractarianism had been taken to the established settler colonies of Canada and Australia, as well as to the United States, soon after their enunciation in the early 1830s, but it was Africa—seen as exotic, pagan, and deadly—which captured the imagination of mid-Victorian minds and convinced many to dedicate their lives and resources, as Livingstone himself would later say, "to heal this open sore" that was the "dark continent."[24] Among those willing to strike out in pursuit of Africa's redemption were some of the followers of the Oxford men.

In 1857, in the midst of a cross-country tour in which he recounted his recent missionary exploits, Livingstone gave a speech at Cambridge appealing to the hundreds of undergraduates in attendance to help him keep Africa open for commerce and Christianity. "Do not let it be shut again!"[25] he implored his rapt listeners. This inspirational speech began the process whereby Cambridge, Oxford, and Durham Universities banded together to form a missionary society that sent its first representatives to central Africa three years later.

The Universities Mission to Central Africa (UMCA), as the society was called, patterned itself consciously on the principles of the Oxford Movement; its first missionary leader, Charles Mackenzie, thought himself a Tractarian missionary bishop. Although loss of life dominated the UMCA's initial foray into Africa, the mission's commitment to engendering Anglo-Catholicism on the banks of the Zambezi River had a lasting impression on the African missionary Church, as well as on British missionary culture generally.

The story of Livingstone's Zambezi expedition to which the UMCA joined itself in 1860 has been told well and needs no great elaboration.[26] However, in the words of Owen Chadwick, "there was much in it of the Oxford Movement,"[27] and it is those features, of course, which most concern us here.

Pusey and Keble supported the UMCA from the outset. The infant mission was committed, in its own words, to "true religion" and would operate "with a Bishop at [its] head."[28] Robert Gray, the remarkably energetic bishop of Cape Town, took a leading role in organizing the UMCA. He was insistent upon the need for a bishop to preside over the new mission, and the diocese which was expected to follow. While home in England during the autumn of 1858 Gray met with Keble and conversed about "missionary bishops . . . , and the principles to guide one in the future expansion of the African Church."[29] The stated desire for a bishop to preside over the UMCA was in marked contrast to the business-like way in which some of the older, established missionary societies operated. For bodies such as the SPCK and the London Missionary Society (LMS), boards of directors were employed to oversee operations. Not so for the UMCA, for whom the consecration of a bishop was a *sine qua non* of its as yet brief existence.

Gray's persistence in pressing for a bishop paid off in the spring of 1859 when he was informed by Lord Derby's government that the UMCA's ecclesiastical plan met with its approval. As Gray wrote happily in a letter to Pusey: "There is nothing to prevent me and my suffragans from consecrating what bishops we like for the Interior of Africa, in my own Cathedral in Cape Town."[30] The news was precisely what Pusey had hoped for, and he was highly gratified by the prospect of the UMCA's establishment on the Tractarian principles he had articulated in 1838. All that was needed now was the right man for the job. Who would be the UMCA's first bishop?

That man was Charles Mackenzie, archdeacon of Natal and late of Caius College, Cambridge. Mackenzie, young, healthy, and determined, had gone out to Africa in 1855. He was a High Churchman and keenly receptive to the message of the Oxford Movement as delivered by Pusey and Keble. In choosing Mackenzie to be the Church of England's first missionary bishop, Gray of Cape Town made clear his own brand of high churchmanship, as well as providing the UMCA with a reasonably experienced Africa hand. Mackenzie's enthusiasm for the task of planting a mission in central Africa was boundless. "We are more popular in the country," he wrote enthusiastically to Samuel Wilberforce, bishop of Oxford, "than any other mission ever was, I believe."[31] Mackenzie would need every ounce of this enthusiasm once he and his six UMCA colleagues met up with Livingstone's Zambezi Expedition at the Kongone mouth of the great river on Africa's east coast in February 1861.

Over the course of the next year the UMCA would establish a mission at Magomero, deep in the south-central African hinterland, maintain a strained but workable relationship with the irascible Livingstone, who at this point in his career had come to much prefer African colleagues to British ones, and tragically, bury its leader and bishop. Mackenzie died on January 30, 1862, after a three-week, malaria-filled wait for Livingstone in an ill-fated rendezvous attempt at the confluence of the Shire and Ruo Rivers, tributaries of the Zambezi. Brandishing his Bible and a copy of Keble's *The Christian Year,* Mackenzie and his fellow missionaries had managed during their brief time up-country to establish a mission station, commence work on a permanent church, institute the daily office, and in what would prove to be a highly controversial move, engage in armed combat against slave-raiders. Apart from the fighting—which would shortly prove almost disabling to the UMCA—under Mackenzie's Tractarian-style direction, Magomero gradually had become the kind of mission envisaged by Pusey, Keble, Gray, and the many others who had lent their support to the project from the moment it had come into prospect back in 1857. But guns and the Cross, always an uneasy partnership, had joined forces along the Zambezi, and once this was known in England the UMCA came in for a severe rebuke by many of its former supporters, including, most notably, Pusey.

In July 1862, a mass meeting was held in Oxford to disseminate publicly the details of the UMCA's short history. Mackenzie's tragic death dominated the proceedings, but of almost equal importance was the description of the Mission's martial activities. The outrage over gun-carrying missionaries—which included Bishop Mackenzie—was acute and among the many voices raised in protest was Pusey's. "It seems to me a frightful thing," lamented the esteemed Regius Professor of Hebrew to the hundreds gathered in the Sheldonian Theatre, "that the messengers of the Gospel of peace should in any way be connected, even by their presence, with the shedding of human blood."[32] The leader of the Anglo-Catholics had spoken; the most prominent living representative of the Oxford Movement had cast judgment over the Movement's missionary progeny. The UMCA's future looked bleak, indeed.

However, over the next few years the UMCA managed to overcome its manifestly disastrous start. Pusey's criticism, while harsh, was also a corrective. The Mission headquarters soon moved to the safer confines of Zanzibar—away from the violence-inducing territorial frontlines of slave-raiding, although placed now ironically at the historic heart of the Indian Ocean slave trade. Gradually the UMCA became a strong missionary society by the end of the nineteenth century and maintained a Tractarian ethos while doing its work in east and south-central Africa well into the twentieth. Keble and Pusey would have been well pleased.

The UMCA was easily the most ambitious and romantic endeavor undertaken by those Victorian churchmen committed both to missionary outreach and to the principles of the Oxford Movement. Africa seemed to ask for the greatest potential sacrifice, and in the person of Bishop Mackenzie, the ultimate sacrifice was made.[33] But while the UMCA epitomizes Tractarian missionary history of the heroic type, a less dramatic brand of mission work can be found in the settler colonies of Canada and Australia, and in the former colonies now comprising the United States. In these places we see, too, a greater elaboration of the kind of intra-Church controversy that was a constant feature of domestic Anglicanism during the Victorian period.

The precepts of the Oxford Movement were introduced to Upper Canada (today's Ontario) by John Strachan, first bishop of Toronto, in the 1830s. Strachan was a High Churchman of the old school and in the years before the Movement's catholic bias became demonstrably Roman supported strongly the work of the Oxford men. Strachan wished to see Church principles of the kind enunciated by the Tractarians lay hold of the young province of Upper Canada and shape its religious ethos. The Church of England in Upper Canada was nominally established during the first half of the nineteenth century, and in defending its position Strachan became equal parts politician and churchman in a career that spanned the years leading up to Canadian Confederation in 1867.

Strachan's battles with the Methodists, as well as other denominations, in the highly charged Protestant world of nineteenth-century Ontario has been well documented and need concern us only incidentally here.[34] More to the point were Strachan's fiery relations with many other Anglicans and what these can tell us about the influence of Tractarianism on the Upper Canadian frontier.

A Presbyterian educated at St. Andrew's University, Strachan emigrated to Upper Canada from Scotland as a young man in 1799. Living in Kingston, he tutored children and then, after joining the Church of England to advance his career, became a missionary in the eastern part of the province. He was ordained in 1803 and in 1812 moved to York (later Toronto), the provincial capital, to assume its rectorship. He took a leading role in York during the War of 1812, during which he reaffirmed his staunch loyalty to the British Crown. Afterward his influence on local church and political affairs increased steadily, especially his defense of the Church of England's putative privileged position in the colony, which included a large land grant called the Clergy Reserves. Strachan became an executive and a legislative councillor and then, in 1839, bishop of Toronto, a preferment he held until his death in 1867.[35]

Strachan's attraction to the Oxford Movement issued from his desire to see a "true Church" established in Upper Canada.[36] To that end while in England during the summer of 1839 awaiting his consecration as Toronto's bishop, Strachan wrote to Newman requesting a meeting with him and the other leading Tractarians.[37] Newman responded favorably, and a meeting was scheduled tentatively for London prior to Strachan's return to Canada. Alas, the meeting did not take place owing to conflicting travel plans. Nevertheless, from that point until 1841 Strachan could see only good in the message of the Tractarians and sought to inculcate sound Church principles in the clergy of his diocese and beyond.[38]

Strachan's admiration for the Tractarians continued until the 1841 publication of Newman's *Tract 90*. But from that point Strachan's disaffection grew, reaching its climax when Newman departed the Church of England for Rome in 1845. The Tractarians had achieved much in Strachan's view, but as he wrote scathingly to a friend, this achievement did "not excuse the insidious proceedings of Mr. Newman and his Party—whose conduct appears to be a sort of insanity—we are well rid of such men that have proved themselves totally unequal to the crisis and unworthy of confidence."[39]

Strachan's personal antipathy toward Newman and some elements of Tractarianism did not, however, diminish his determination to ensure the preeminence of "Z"-style High Church principles in Upper Canada, along with the political preeminence of the Church of England. His hearty establishmentarianism also put him at odds with the extreme end of Tractarian thinking, whose high priest, Hurrell Froude, had left behind at his death the charge that the English establishment should be abolished to permit the replacement of the compromised Anglican church with a "real one."[40]

Strachan eventually lost his battle with the forces of political reform. The Clergy Reserves were secularized in 1854, marking formally the disestablishment of the Church of England in the province, an establishment that had never been more than partial and uneasy. Strachan's long interest in and fight for confessional Anglican education was capped with the founding of Trinity College in 1852, a High Church institution that was to rival the secular University of Toronto, begun by Strachan himself in 1827 as King's College but since removed from Anglican control by the provincial legislature.

Within the Church of England in Upper Canada party conflict remained rife and manifested itself most visibly in the hotly contested field of education. The Irish-born evangelical Benjamin Cronyn, elected bishop of Huron in 1857, disagreed fundamentally with Strachan's high churchmanship and the Anglo-Catholic nature of Trinity College. Cronyn countered Strachan's influence by establishing the evangelical Huron College in London, Ontario, in 1863. Charges and denunciations flew back and forth between the two men and their followers. As John Webster Grant observes: "Eventually, the church had not only rival

theological colleges and private schools but competing missionary societies, hymn-books, and even Sunday school lessons."[41]

In Upper Canada (Canada West after the 1841 union of Upper and
Lower Canada and the creation of the Province of Canada) Anglo-Catholic parishes were never as numerous as evangelical, but their very existence was bound to provoke conflict in the overwhelmingly Protestant
province. Of course, the English-French, Protestant-Catholic cleavage at
the heart of nineteenth-century Canadian politics colored heavily the
public's view of internal Church and interdenominational conflict. For
Anglo-Catholics, some degree of public animosity became an expected
hazard of their churchmanship. Regardless, the influence of the Oxford
Movement remained pronounced in nineteenth-century Ontario and
shaped a tradition of Canadian colonial Tractarianism.[42]

Elsewhere in the British Empire Tractarianism had a similarly divisive effect. In Australia, the Oxford Movement engendered a high level
of controversy. Like the Church of England in Upper Canada, Anglicans
in the largest Australian colony of New South Wales were given a privileged position in law through the establishment of the Church and
Schools Corporation in 1825 and its grant to the Church of one-seventh
of the land in the colony. And, as in Upper Canada, opposition by other
Protestants to the Church of England's privileged position was swift in
coming. In fact, the opposition was so strong and so sustained that the
Imperial government decided only four years later to suspend the
Church and Schools Corporation. Two years after that, in 1831, the Corporation was ended altogether.

Presiding over the Anglican Church in New South Wales was William Grant Broughton, archdeacon.[43] The government's abandonment
of the establishment principle made it clear to Broughton that in order
for the Church to survive it would have to reduce its popular opposition
significantly. Doing so, however, was no easy task, and Broughton found
himself unable to chart a consistent course in the midst of the myriad
demands and details of his heavily administrative archdeaconry—and in
a climate where Anglicanism was being treated as one Protestant sect
among many. For three years he soldiered on and then finally sought a
reprieve in his native England in 1834.

In that year the Oxford Movement was gathering momentum. The *Tracts for the Times* were being published, and Broughton quickly became caught up in the Tractarians' enthusiasm for Church renewal and a right reading of the establishment principle. He was introduced to the strong Tractarian supporter, Edward Coleridge—Eton master and cousin of the bishop of the West Indies with whom Froude was shortly to have a strained relationship—and their burgeoning friendship was vital to Broughton's imbibing the Tractarian position on the Church.

Before returning to the South Pacific in 1836 Broughton was consecrated bishop of Australia. Thus elevated, and fortified with the teachings of the Oxford Movement, the new bishop plunged back into the religious and political scene of his adopted home.

Broughton anchored himself in the issue of Anglican education, arguing for exclusive control based not on the old constitutional guarantees of the Act of Settlement and the Coronation oath, but on the Church and theological grounds delineated by the Tractarians. As in Canada, control over education was eventually secularized in Australia, but Broughton continued to cling to the message of the Oxford Movement regardless of the changes in temporal governance. As his diocese grew in population, the clergy who came to New South Wales were sometimes in sympathy with the Tractarian view, although not enough of them to satisfy Broughton. As he requested in a letter to Coleridge: "Your introduction of [Newman's] name reminds me to say that if I might make choice of my fellow labourers, they should be from this school. They take, I think, the most just and comprehensive view of the true constitution of our Church."[44]

Broughton's position provoked severe opposition both among evangelical and latitudinarian Anglicans and from the liberal press, who found his exalted view of the Church anachronistic and utterly unsuited to the rough and ready Australian frontier. Broughton, however, was so sure of his own churchmanship and so relentless in maintaining and then enlarging the diocesan system in the 1840s, that out of his own diocese of Australia were spawned those of Tasmania, Adelaide, Melbourne, Newcastle, and Sydney.

Broughton died in 1853, his strongly held Tractarianism undiminished to the end, although he, like Strachan, was outraged by Newman's conversion. Broughton was more responsible than anyone else for trans-planting the ideas of the Oxford Movement to the Antipodes. Certainly he did much to forward the need for colonial bishoprics and was a lead-ing proponent of the Colonial Bishoprics' Fund, both in Australia and elsewhere.

From its inception in 1841, the Colonial Bishoprics' Fund was vital to the spread of the Church of England throughout the empire. Bishop Blomfield of London was primarily responsible for creating the fund as a means of establishing bishoprics in colonies where the state no longer provided endowments. Periodic and successful public appeals were made in support of the fund. At one such appeal at Westminster Abbey in 1847 the enthusiasm for missions was palpable, if not exaggerated: "Surely there has not been such a Communion seen in this our day, nor, as we believe, for ages in the Church here in England."[45] The belief that the Anglican Church had entered a new missionary era was real, and the evidence for it kept arriving from colonies such as India, Canada, Austra-lia, and later, from Africa, as we have already seen in part.

Pusey, as the most interested of the leading Tractarians in missions, was fully supportive of the Colonial Bishoprics' Fund during its initial phase. But his ardor for the fund began to cool once the colonial Churches and bishops began to move away from metropolitan control and toward colonial synods. Newman had once protested vigorously in-dividual societal (that is to say, CMS) control over missionaries as dam-aging to the authority and consecration of the Church. Now in the late 1840s Pusey began to see in the Colonial Bishoprics' Fund, and its rela-tions with the SPG in particular, the same incremental incursion into the rightful prerogatives of the Church.

But more important still was Pusey's concern over the continuing Erastianism that made for two levels of authority for colonial bishops: local and metropolitan. This division could and did result in severe schism, especially in South Africa in the 1860s.

The Colenso case, as the generative event of this schism is known, was brought about when William Colenso, first bishop of Natal, was tried for heresy in 1863, a charge formally brought against him by Bishop Gray, metropolitan of the ecclesiastical province of South Africa. A long-time missionary among the Zulu, Colenso was theologically liberal by the standards of the time and owed much to his reading of one of the founders of Christian socialism, F. D. Maurice. Colenso's liberal position on baptismal regeneration and his insistence on interpreting Zulu culture through the lens of natural religion and rationality came into conflict with the prevailing Calvinistic view held of native Africans, a view shared by the majority of Anglican missionaries in South Africa—pansinfulness. For maintaining an opposing stance, Colenso was duly deposed by Gray's consistorial court made up of the suffragan bishops of the province. Controversially, Colenso appealed the decision, not to an ecclesiastical body, but rather to a civil one, the Judicial Committee of the Privy Council in London. He did so because of the ongoing dispute over diocesan authority. Colenso believed that his position as the consecrated bishop of Natal put him outside Gray's authority. In 1865, the Privy Council agreed with Colenso. Gray responded by excommunicating Colenso and beginning a search for a new diocesan for Natal. Incensed, Colenso continued to conduct services in Durban and at the cathedral in Pietermaritzburg. He then brought suit against the Colonial Bishoprics' Fund, which had stopped paying his annual income when he took his case to a secular court, and won. The Fund was then forced to resume its payments by order of the Chancery Court.[46] Thus buffeted by controversy the Church in South Africa split. Colenso died in 1883. He spent the last years of his life working tirelessly, and with some success, for the better treatment of native Africans by their colonial masters.

For Pusey, the Colenso imbroglio brought into sharp relief the meddling hand of the state made normative by the existence of the establishment, and he continued to question its necessity, especially the power of episcopal appointment overseas. Secondarily, Pusey wondered at metropolitan jurisdiction once the appointment had been made. The vital Tractarian precept of episcopal authority was preeminent in his mind, and he strove to embolden Gray to defy the "infidel Privy Council['s]" encroachment on the sacred authority of the Church.[47]

The Colenso controversy came in the midst of the upheaval in Church and theological affairs that characterized Anglicanism in the early to mid-nineteenth century. Frances Knight does not exaggerate when describing the years 1800–1870 in the life of the Church of England as marking "a transformation more rapid, dramatic and enduring than any which it had experienced since the Reformation."[48] Tensions ran high across the spectrum of issues that now confronted the Church: industrialization, Erastianism, denominationalism, biblical higher criticism, missions, and others. In this way the intensity with which the participants in the Colenso case conducted their campaigns is further illustrative of the ferocity with which these issues were fought over at this time. Pusey and those who shared his churchmanship injected a Tractarian zealotry into their defense of the Church's prerogatives wherever these might be under attack—from Leeds to Cape Town.

Pusey's concern for the colonial Church remained strong until his death. He questioned the move to synods in many colonies because it meant the introduction of laymen into what should be, and at home had always been, sacred deliberations. Leading colonial bishops— Strachan and Broughton especially—considered it necessary to include laymen in such deliberations, since without state aid popular support was vital to the health of their Churches. But Pusey was not won over by this argument, mostly because of its potentially harmful effects at home in the form of a revived Convocation—a body that had not been sanctioned since 1717 when it had been suppressed by the disaffected and mostly absent King George I. "I look with terror," Pusey wrote to Keble, "on any admission of laity into *Synods*. It at once invests them with an ecclesiastical office, which will develop itself sooner or later, I believe, to the destruction of the Faith."[49]

Of course, a diminution of the exalted and sacred order of bishop, priest, and deacon, an order that was a central tenet of Tractarianism, was unacceptable to Pusey. The reality of the colonial Church apparently made it necessary, but in his view, the position was deeply erroneous. He corresponded with many overseas bishops on this point but they were unable to dissuade him from his considered view. One plan of Pusey's that did meet with their approval, however, was his idea for a missionary college in Oxford. But approval was not forthcoming from Pusey's own bishop, Richard Bagot, who saw in such a college another means to engender party strife within the university. Nevertheless, the college did materialize in 1848 as St. Augustine's College, Canterbury. Edward Coleridge, Eton master, once again had shown his devotion to missions by campaigning for its creation.[50] But the college was never a success, mostly because the colonial Church had begun to rely increasingly on home-grown clergy. As well, native Englishmen entering the Church usually desired the relative security and prestige of a local parish, not, say, the backwoods of Upper Canada or the barren wastes of western Australia.[51]

Pusey's concern for the colonial Church of England was a natural part of his catholicity. So, too, was that expressed for the Episcopal Church in the former British colonies now reconstituted as the United States of America. While the American Church was not "colonial" in the sense of its cousin to the north, the impact of the Oxford Movement on it was similarly controversial and important.

While America may have been "The City on the Hill" for its Puritan founders, to churchmen it was less grand a place, a place where the established faith could be planted like any other. New England was dominated by the Puritans but elsewhere the Church of England quickly became a significant religious presence in early America. From 1691 on it was the established Church in Virginia, Maryland, Georgia, and the Carolinas. Admittedly, such a status did not mean a great deal in the frontier world of seventeenth-century America, where parishes were enormous, the population small, and the bishop nonresident. Indeed no colonial bishop for America was ever named, and after 1700 talk of one became tied up in fears that a colonial bishop would act as a Trojan horse, potentially limiting the political freedom of the colonies.[52] The Church grew nonetheless, and by the middle of the eighteenth century it had become an important part of the religious fabric of many of the Thirteen Colonies, with variations in strength depending upon place and time.

The War of Independence shattered the Church of England's position in early America. British loyalism was demonstrated most visibly by Anglicans, and they suffered greatly for their continuing support of the British Crown. The SPG and the bishop of London, who had supported and overseen the American Church, were cut off by the war, and the local clergy and laity were left abandoned and impoverished. On the other hand, however, there were many churchmen who supported the American rebels. The history of the Church of England during the revolutionary period, therefore, is a complicated one.[53]

In 1783, once peace had been restored, the former Church of England in America renamed itself the Protestant Episcopal Church and began a new chapter in its history. The next year at Philadelphia a convention was held in order to frame a constitution by which this new episcopal body would govern itself. The convention saw the cooperation of both clergy and laity—a first in Anglican history—and pledged itself to be in agreement with the doctrine and worship of the Church of England. William White, a thirty-six-year-old rector from Philadelphia, was the convention's guiding spirit. Many issues—a set of canons, a prayer book, and so on—remained outstanding following the Philadelphia meeting and would take until 1789 to resolve. But the new United States of America had a new Protestant Church based on ancient episcopal principles.

In the early part of the nineteenth century the Episcopal Church engaged in an intense missionary program, pushing west to the Ohio Valley along with the thousands of settlers. This physical expansion was vital to renewing the health of the American Church. Meanwhile, the Oxford Movement was about to move into the consciousness of the American Church, bringing with it an intellectual and spiritual change equal in power to that engendered by the westward trek.

Keble's *The Christian Year* first appeared in the United States in 1834; the *Tracts for the Times* followed in 1839. The ground they fell upon was already churned up by the roil of High Church and Low Church disputes which had coursed through Episcopalianism in a way not unlike that found in England—although without an establishment in the United States there was no intrinsic political element to them. The Oxford Movement inflamed these disputes, and for some detractors *Tract 90* unmasked the Tractarians as the closet Romanists they were assumed to be. The evangelical bishop of Ohio, Charles McIlvaine, led the charge against the Oxford men: "The whole system, you see, is one of church instead of Christ; priest instead of Gospel; concealment of truth instead of 'manifestation of truth'; ignorant superstition instead of enlightened faith; bondage where we are promised liberty."[54] Sides had been taken, and the battle was well and truly joined.

The General Seminary in the old loyalist redoubt of New York City became the center for Tractarian controversy, especially over the ordination of one of its leading graduates, Arthur Carey, in 1843. Carey admired deeply the message and the men of the Oxford Movement, especially Newman, and on the eve of his ordination his controversial position was called into question by the bishop of New York, Benjamin Onderdonk, who convened a special committee of eight assessors to examine Carey as to his Protestant soundness. The examination had about it the air of a mock trial, although the intention of the bishop and the eight assessors was deadly serious. Carey survived the ordeal and Onderdonk decided to ordain him in short order. The consequent service of ordination was interrupted, however, by the joint protest of two of the assessors, who declared that Carey held "sentiments not conformable to the doctrines of the Protestant Episcopal Church in the United States of America, and in too close conformity with the Church of Rome."[55] Onderdonk rejected the protest, however, and Carey was duly ordained deacon.

The Carey case brought tensions over Tractarianism within the Episcopal Church to the boiling point, and they spilled over at the General Convention held the following year, 1844. The Seminary's role in sponsoring Tractarianism, as its opponents saw it to be doing, was denounced by Bishop McIlvaine and others. Their intense protest put the Seminary's future in peril, but the Convention did not bow to their demands for a clear denunciation of the Oxford Movement. Instead, after much debate, the House of Bishops issued an irenicon concluding "that neither Romanists on the one hand, nor enemies of the Episcopal Church on the other, may have cause to boast that we have departed in the slightest degree from the spirit and principles of the Reformation, as exemplified by the Church of England."[56] Low Churchmen were mollified, and their protests over the dangerously infectious Tractarianism ebbed.

After 1845 and Newman's conversion, defections to Rome afflicted the Episcopal Church as they did in England, Australia, Canada, and elsewhere. The intensity of the Carey crisis, however, was not relived in any other episode. Indeed, the American experience is exceptional in that once the doctrinal controversy passed in 1843–44 subsequent issues did not carry with them the extreme bitterness that the ongoing disputes over different brands of churchmanship brought in the other areas of the Anglican communion examined here. This exceptionalism is due mostly to the absence of the Episcopal Church's establishment or semi-establishment in the United States. Whereas in England, Canada, and Australia, the Church's status was inherently political, the American Episcopal Church was outside this particularly explosive matrix where the essence of the society in question was under constant review and the main features of it—such as public education—were steadily fought over.

In other ways, however, the impact of the Oxford Movement on the Episcopal Church mirrored that found elsewhere. The form of the liturgy elicited new and sustained interest; the Eucharist was celebrated more frequently in response to Pusey's emphasis on the centrality of it to the right-minded Christian community;[57] clerical vestments, (choral) music, and church design all acquired a new importance. In New York City the Gothic Trinity Church rose in 1846 and became a benchmark of design for self-consciously Tractarian architects, congregations, and clergy, such as John Henry Hobart.[58]

Party spirit remained high within the Episcopal Church for most of the nineteenth century. Different magazines served different constituencies. *The Churchman* was the voice of High Churchmen and Tractarians. A similar dichotomy took place in educational and outreach societies. In all of these areas the American experience of Tractarianism conformed to the patterns seen in other areas influenced greatly by the Oxford Movement.

The Oxford Movement's success in exporting its ideas is unsurprising, given that it moved in train with Britain's national extroversion throughout the Victorian era. While political events and personal crises flowed together to spawn the Movement, the course that it would run at home and then abroad was far from the minds of its founders in the yeasty days of 1833. But over the next twelve years and beyond Tractarianism engendered a fundamental reassessment of all facets of the Church of England. For missions, the Oxford Movement reasserted the primacy of the Church to Christianity's proper expansion. The Tractarians disagreed profoundly with the apparently less than holy and orderly assortment of missionary societies that had sprung up in great profusion in the late-eighteenth and early-nineteenth centuries. Key to the Tractarian apprehension of the missionary task was the spread of Church principles upon which a proper extension of the church catholic could be made. Of course, in the complicated ecclesiastical world of establishments, colonies, and interested parties of one sort or another, the essentials of the Tractarian project were not always the axis upon which the variously located debates hinged. Yet the Tractarians, especially Pusey, remained steady in their advocacy of a singularly acceptable kind of missionary activity, and the consequences of this sturdy stance are there to be observed wherever the Tractarian message was spread. Central Africa, Canada, Australia, the United States, in each of these places the Oxford Movement's impact on the mid-nineteenth-century Church of England was important and transforming. In its contact with these new societies, the movement functioned in its own terms as a missionary Church. "The Church is," declared Pusey, "in prophecy as in history and fact, *the* preacher of the Gospel."[59] If the Tractarians brought this belief a little closer to pass, then they fulfilled their self-defined missionary mandate.

Afterword

*E*ven though the formal phase of the Oxford Movement ended in 1845 with Newman's conversion, the ideas of the Tractarians lived on. Their position on church and state was important to the ongoing nineteenth-century debate over the nature of the British establishment, while their revival of catholic practices marked Anglican modes of liturgical worship, something that continues today. In the realm of society, the Anglo-Catholic inheritors of the Tractarians sponsored a particular kind of Social Christianity that echoed Pusey's teaching on eucharistic communitarianism, one that would reach its apogee in the first decades of the twentieth century under the leadership domestically of Charles Gore, theologian and sometime bishop of Oxford, and in the colonial church by Frank Weston, bishop of Zanzibar. Indeed, so pronounced was the impact of Anglo-Catholicism that Adrian Hastings suggests persuasively that by 1900 it was behind "almost all Christian socialism."[1] Such a development surely would have surprised—and perhaps even alarmed—Newman, Keble, and Froude, although Pusey probably would have been gratified. Social Christianity's decline in the years following the Second World War meant that Anglo-Catholicism's social project declined in its broader impact too.[2] The emergence of the welfare state and the dominance of its secular prescriptions for how to combat poverty and dispossession pushed Social Christianity to society's margins, a position that it continues to occupy.

A broad and thematic study such as this one leaves many questions unanswered. Much more needs to be known about the nature of Tractarianism's impact on local history, for instance, something a concentrated study of various parish records might supply. Another area on which to focus is the colonial church and how it defined and organized itself within the new societies of the expanding British Empire. What can a close study of Tractarianism abroad teach us about its spread and impact outside Britain? Similarly, additional work in gender history would enlarge our understanding of the Oxford Movement's impact on Victorian women. Sexuality and the Tractarians is another area that would benefit from modern scholarship. A sensitive probing of the issues of homosexuality, virginity, and celibacy potentially could uncover much about the motivations and prejudices of some of the original Tractarians and their followers.

In recent years the rise of political, social, and religious conservatism in much of the developed world has renewed the currency of Anglo-Catholicism's social message. In light of the harsh criticism leveled by many against statist prescriptions for narrowing the gap between rich and poor, Anglo-Catholicism's ideas on community and poverty reduction have become more appealing to various churches and social-welfare advocates. Whether or not the heirs of the Oxford Movement will reemerge as a powerful force within the greatly diminished ranks of Social Christianity, is yet to be seen, as is the fate of Social Christianity itself. Thus as the founding of the Oxford Movement approaches the second century mark, many questions remain about its impact and legacy. Perhaps the deepest one is that which animated the original Tractarians themselves at the outset of the movement back in 1833: Whither the place of the Church in the modern world?

Notes

Preface and Acknowledgments

1. These dates are those used by R. W. Church in his classic account, *The Oxford Movement: Twelve Years, 1833–1845* (London: Macmillan, 1891).

2. Lawrence Crumb has compiled a bibliography of works on the Oxford Movement that numbers over 7500 entries. See Lawrence N. Crumb, *The Oxford Movement and Its Leaders: A Bibliography of Secondary and Lesser Primary Sources* (Metuchen, N.J.: American Theological Library Association, Scarecrow Press, 1988); *Supplement* (1993).

Chapter 1

1. Owen Chadwick, *The Spirit of the Oxford Movement: Tractarian Essays* (Cambridge: Cambridge University Press, 1990), 2.

2. Terence Kenny, *The Political Thought of John Henry Newman* (London: Longmans, Green, 1957); J.H.L. Rowlands, *Church, State and Society: The Attitudes of John Keble, Richard Hurrell Froude and John Henry Newman, 1827–1845* (Worthing, West Sussex: Churchman Publishing, 1989); Peter B. Nockles, *The Oxford Movement in Context: Anglican High Churchmanship, 1760–1857* (Cambridge: Cambridge University Press, 1994).

3. R. W. Church, *The Oxford Movement: Twelve Years, 1833–1845* (London: Macmillan, 1891). See, also, the 1970 edition, edited by Geoffrey Best for the University of Chicago Press, and David Newsome, *The Parting of Friends: A Study of the Wilburforces and Henry Manning* (London: J. Murray, 1966). Given the scope of this book I decided that I would adopt Church's twelve-year duration as a guide because it offered the clearest chronology of the most important events of the Movement.

4. J.C.D. Clark, *English Society, 1688–1832* (Cambridge: Cambridge University Press, 1985), 375. Also see Geoffrey Best, "The Constitutional Revolution, 1828–32, and Its Consequences for the Established Church," *Theology* 62, no. 463 (1959): 226–50.

5. Wendy Hinde, *Catholic Emancipation: A Shake to Men's Minds* (Oxford: Basil Blackwell, 1992), iv.

6. See G.I.T. Machin, *The Catholic Question in English Politics, 1820 to 1830* (Oxford: Clarendon Press, 1964).

7. Quoted in Ian Ker, *John Henry Newman: A Biography* (Oxford: Oxford University Press, 1988), 33.

8. Quoted in Georgina Battiscombe, *John Keble: A Study in Limitations* (London: Constable, 1963), 124.

9. See Piers Brendon, *Hurrell Froude and the Oxford Movement* (London: Paul Elek, 1974), 94–96.

10. J. H. Newman to Henry Wilberforce, July 16, 1833, in *The Letters and Diaries of John Henry Newman*, vol. 4, ed. Ian Ker and Thomas Gornall (Oxford: Clarendon Press, 1980), 9.

11. Quoted in Brendon, *Hurrell Froude*, 122.

12. John Henry Newman, *Apologia Pro Vita Sua*, ed. Martin J. Svaglic (Oxford: Clarendon Press, 1967), 43.

13. For a detailed study, see Robin Sharwood, "The Oriel Common Room of 1833," in *Colonial Tractarians: The Oxford Movement in Australia*, ed. Brian Porter (Melbourne: Joint Board of Christian Education, 1989), 145–60.

14. Ker, *John Henry Newman*, 15–18.

15. Newman, *Apologia*, 11.

16. Ibid., 39.

17. Quoted in Brendon, *Hurrell Froude*, 46.

18. Nockles, *Oxford Movement in Context*, 25–26.

19. Newman's youthful evangelicalism is described well in Sheridan Gilley, *Newman and His Age* (London: Darton, Longman and Todd, 1990), chap. 2.

20. Henry Liddon, quoted in Bernard M.G. Reardon, *From Coleridge to Gore: A Century of Religious Thought in Britain* (London: Longman, 1971), 23.

21. See Newman, *Apologia*, 20–24; Gilley, *Newman and His Age*, chap. 5.

22. *The Letters and Diaries of John Henry Newman*, vol. 2, ed. Ian Ker and Thomas Gornall (Oxford: Clarendon Press, 1979), 218.

23. Reardon, *From Coleridge to Gore*, 43.

24. *John Henry Newman: Autobiographical Writings*, ed. Henry Tristram (London: Macmillan, 1956), 185.

25. Newman, *Apologia*, 52.

26. Clark, *English Society*, 415.

27. J. H. Newman to H. A. Woodgate, August 7, 1833, in Newman, *Letters and Diaries*, 4:27.

28. Quoted in Battiscombe, *John Keble*, 157.

29. J. H. Newman to Hugh James Rose, December 15, 1833, in Newman, *Letters and Diaries*, 4:143.

30. Ibid., 160.

31. [J. H. Newman], *Tracts for the Times*, no. 2, "The Catholic Church" (1833), 2.

32. Ibid., 4.

33. [John Keble], *Tracts for the Times*, no. 4, "Adherence to the Apostolical Succession the Safest Course" (1833), 7.

34. [R. Hurrell Froude], *Tracts for the Times*, no. 9, "On Shortening the Church Services" (1833), 1–3.

35. Newman, *Apologia*, 64.

36. [J. H. Newman], *Tracts for the Times*, no. 38, "Via Media—No. I," and no. 41, "Via Media—No. II," (1834).

37. John William Bowden to J. H. Newman, July 14, 1834, in Newman, *Letters and Diaries*, 4:304.

38. See Richard Allen Soloway, *Prelates and People: Ecclesiastical Social Thought in England, 1783–1852* (London: Routledge and Kegan Paul, 1969).

39. [R. H. Froude], *Tracts for the Times,* no. 59, "Church and State" (1835), 1.

40. Ibid., 2.

41. Quoted in David Cecil, *Melbourne* (London: The Reprint Society, 1955), 245.

42. Nathaniel Teich, "*The British Critic,*" in *British Literary Magazines: The Romantic Age, 1789–1836,* ed. Alvin Sullivan (Westport, Conn.: Greenwood Press, 1983), 57.

43. S. W. Wilberforce to J. H. Newman, July 19, 1838, "*British Critic, 1836–1841,*" Pusey MSS, Pusey House, Oxford.

44. Peter B. Nockles, "Continuity and Change in British High Churchmanship, 1792–1850" (D.Phil. thesis, University of Oxford, 1982), xii.

45. [Thomas Mozley], "Church and King," *British Critic* 25 (April 1839): 321.

46. Ibid., 367.

47. W. E. Gladstone, *The State in Its Relations with the Church,* 4th ed. (London: J. Murray, 1841), 1:4.

48. See Richard J. Helmstadter, "Conscience and Politics: Gladstone's First Book," in *The Gladstonian Turn of Mind,* ed. Bruce L. Kinzer (Toronto: University of Toronto Press, 1985), 3–42.

49. *The Gladstone Diaries,* ed. M.R.D. Foot and H.C.G. Matthew, vol. 3 (Oxford: Clarendon Press, 1974), May 9, 1841.

50. Agatha Ramm, "Gladstone's Religion," *The Historical Journal* 28, no. 2 (1985): 327–40; Perry Butler, *Gladstone Church, State, and Tractarianism: A Study of His Religious Ideas and Attitudes, 1809–1859* (Oxford: Clarendon Press, 1982).

51. Robert Blake, *Disraeli* (New York: St. Martin's Press, 1967), 168.

52. Ibid., 171.

53. Benjamin Disraeli, *Coningsby, Or the New Generation,* ed. Thom Braun (Markham, Ont.: Penguin, 1983), 378.

54. Ibid., 377.

55. Benjamin Disraeli, *Sybil, Or the Two Nations,* ed. Sheila M. Smith (New York: Oxford University Press, 1991), 150.

56. Ibid., 107.

57. Sarah Bradford, *Disraeli* (New York: Stein and Day, 1983), 160.

58. Peter G. Cobb, "Leader of the Anglo-Catholics?" in *Pusey Rediscovered,* ed. Perry Butler (London: SPCK, 1983), 349.

59. Quoted in Geoffrey Faber, *Oxford Apostles: A Character Study of the Oxford Movement,* 2d ed. (London: Faber and Faber, 1974), 371.

60. Quoted in H. P. Liddon, *Life of Edward Bouverie Pusey* (London: Longmans, Green, 1893–97), 3:249.

61. Ibid., 4:213.

62. E. B. Pusey, *The Royal Supremacy not an Arbitrary Authority But Limited by the Laws of the Church, of which Kings are Members* (Oxford: John Henry Parker, 1850), 212.

63. Quoted in Chadwick, "The Limitations of Keble," in *The Spirit of the Oxford Movement,* 62.

Chapter 2

1. See, for example, Gordon Rupp, *Religion in England, 1688–1791* (Oxford: Clarendon Press, 1986), and Robert Hole, *Pulpits, Politics and Public Order in England, 1760–1832* (Cambridge: Cambridge University Press, 1989).

2. See Nigel Yates, *Anglican Ritualism in Victorian Britain, 1830–1910* (Oxford: Oxford University Press, 1999). Also see D. G. Paz, *Popular Anti-Catholicism in Mid-Victorian England* (Stanford: Stanford University Press, 1992).

3. See John Shelton Reed, *Glorious Battle: The Cultural Politics of Victorian Anglo-Catholicism* (Nashville: Vanderbilt University Press, 1996), and Arthur Burns, *The Diocesan Revival in the Church of England, c. 1800–1870* (Oxford: Clarendon Press, 1999).

4. J. H. Newman, *Apologia Pro Vita Sua,* ed. Martin J. Svaglic (Oxford: Clarendon Press, 1967), 18.

5. Peter B. Nockles, *The Oxford Movement in Context: Anglican High Churchmanship, 1760–1857* (Cambridge: Cambridge University Press, 1994), and Kenneth Hylson-Smith, *High Churchmanship in the Church of England: From the Sixteenth Century to the Late Twentieth Century* (Edinburgh: T. and T. Clark, 1993).

6. Nockles, *Oxford Movement in Context,* 25–26.

7. Hylson-Smith, *High Churchmanship,* 100.

8. Owen Chadwick, *The Spirit of the Oxford Movement: Tractarian Essays* (Cambridge: Cambridge University Press, 1990), 27.

9. H. J. Rose to J. H. Newman, May 10, 1836, Newman MSS, The Oratory, Birmingham.

10. "Boldness" was a necessary course of action, Newman maintained. J. H. Newman to H. J. Rose, May 11, 1836, in *The Letters and Diaries of John Henry Newman,* vol. 5, ed. Gerard Tracey (Oxford: Clarendon Press, 1995), 295.

11. Quoted in Nockles, *Oxford Movement in Context,* 153.

12. John Oxlee, quoted in ibid., 156.

13. For a detailed treatment of this phenomenon in British society, see D. G. Paz, *Popular Anti-Catholicism in Mid-Victorian England* (Stanford: Stanford University Press, 1992).

14. J.C.D. Clark, *English Society, 1688–1832* (Cambridge: Cambridge University Press, 1985), 272.

15. Quoted in Nockles, *Oxford Movement in Context,* 166.

16. [J. H. Newman], *Tracts for the Times,* no. 71, "On the Controversy with the Romanists" (1835).

17. Ibid., 1, 14.

18. Ibid., 35.

19. In the early years of the nineteenth century the *Critic* had a subscription list of some 3500 names, making it one of the most popular journals in England. Walter Graham, *English Literary Periodicals* (New York: T. Nelson, 1930), 221.

20. *The Letters and Correspondence of John Henry Newman During His Life in the English Church,* ed. Anne Mozley (Oxford: Oxford University Press, 1891), 2:164.

21. Ibid., 122, 92.

22. Ibid., 154.

23. Joshua Watson to J. H. Newman, All Saints' Day, 1837, Newman Papers, "*British Critic,* 1836–1841," Pusey MSS, Pusey House, Oxford.

24. E. R. Houghton, "The *British Critic* and the Oxford Movement" (Charlottesville: Bibliographical Society of the University of Virginia, 1963), 125–27.

25. Sheridan Gilley, *Newman and His Age* (London: Darton, Longman and Todd, 1990), 172.

26. Beverley A.B. Tinsley, "John Henry Newman and the *British Critic*" (Ph.D. diss., Northwestern University, 1972), 126.

27. Peter B. Nockles, "Continuity and Change in British High Churchmanship, 1792–1850" (D.Phil. thesis, University of Oxford, 1982), xii.

28. [Thomas Mozley], "Church and King," *British Critic* 25 (April 1839); [George Bowyer], "Ecclesiastical Discipline," ibid.; [J. H. Newman], "State of Religious Parties," ibid.

29. [Bowyer], "Ecclesiastical Discipline," 427.

30. Quoted in Houghton, "The *British Critic* and the Oxford Movement," 125.

31. Edward Churton to Joshua Watson, February 6, 1843, Churton MSS, Pusey House, Oxford.

32. Quoted in Nockles, *Oxford Movement in Context,* 176.

33. Quoted in ibid., 179.

34. Quoted in ibid., 181.

35. Ibid., 182.

36. Yates, *Anglican Ritualism;* Mats Selen, *The Oxford Movement and Wesleyan Methodism in England, 1833–1882: A Study in Religious Conflict* (Lund: Lund University Press, 1992). See, also, Paul Vaiss, ed., *From Oxford to the People: Reconsidering Newman and the Oxford Movement* (Leominster: Gracewing, 1996).

37. William Palmer, *A Narrative of Events connected with the Publication of the Tracts for the Times,* 2d ed. (London: Mowbray, 1883), 241.

38. This brief biographical sketch relies on Michael Reynolds, *Martyr of Ritualism: Father Mackonochie of St. Alban's, Holborn* (London: Mowbray, 1965).

39. H. P. Liddon, *Life of Edward Bouverie Pusey* (London: Longmans, Green, 1893–97), 4:277.

40. Chadwick, *Spirit of the Oxford Movement,* 1.

41. *The Autobiography of Isaac Williams,* ed. George Prevost (London: Longmans, Green, 1892).

42. John Keble, *National Apostasy,* introduction by Alan M.G. Stephenson (Abingdon, Oxfordshire, 1983), 25.

43. Ibid., 19, 24.

44. Georgina Battiscombe, *John Keble: A Study in Limitations* (London: Constable, 1963), 77.

45. Ibid., 269.

46. Ibid., 312.

47. Quoted in Ian Ker, *John Henry Newman: A Biography* (Oxford: Oxford University Press, 1988), 231.

48. J. H. Newman, *Discussions and Arguments on Various Subjects* (London: Rivington, 1873), 140.

49. Ibid., 146–51.

50. Quoted in Liddon, *Life of Pusey,* 2:140.

51. Yngve Brilioth, *The Anglican Revival* (London: Longmans, Green, 1925), 296.

52. Chadwick, *Spirit of the Oxford Movement,* 39.

53. See Chapter 4.

54. See Nockles, *Oxford Movement in Context,* chap. 5, "Spirituality, Liturgy and Worship," 184–227. Much of what follows is drawn from this chapter.

55. [E. B. Pusey], *Tracts for the Times,* no. 18, "Thoughts on the Benefits of Fasting Enjoined by our Church" (1833), and no. 66, "Supplement to Tract XVIII. On the Benefits of the System of Fasting Prescribed by our Church" (1833).

56. Nockles, *Oxford Movement in Context,* 190.

57. Sheridan Gilley, "John Keble and the Victorian Churching of Romanticism," in *An Infinite Complexity: Essays in Romanticism,* ed. J. R. Watson (Edinburgh: University of Edinburgh Press, 1983), 226–39.

58. John Keble, *The Christian Year* (London: Oxford University Press, 1914), 5.

59. Nockles, *Oxford Movement in Context,* 198.

60. [Isaac Williams], *Tracts for the Times,* no. 80, "On Reserve in Communicating Religious Knowledge" (1837).

61. Ibid., 3.

62. Ibid.

63. Peter Toon, *Evangelical Theology, 1833–1856: A Response to Tractarianism* (London: Marshall, Morgan and Scott, 1979), 133.

64. Quoted in Nockles, *Oxford Movement in Context,* 200.

65. Ibid., 207.

66. James Anthony Froude, the historian and Hurrell Froude's younger brother, came to hold this view of the impact of the Oxford Movement. Herbert Paul, *The Life of Froude,* 2d ed. (London: Pitman, 1906), 24.

67. [J. H. Newman], *Tracts for the Times,* no. 75, "On the Roman Breviary as Embodying the Substance of the Devotional Services of the Church Catholic" (1836), 1.

68. Nockles, *Oxford Movement in Context,* 222.

69. [R. H. Froude], *Tracts for the Times,* no. 63, "The Antiquity of the Existing Liturgies" (1835), 1.

70. Ibid.

71. Nockles, *Oxford Movement in Context,* 225.

72. Quoted in ibid.

73. George William Herring identifies almost one thousand Tractarian clergy active in Anglican parishes in mid-nineteenth-century England. From his unpublished thesis, "Tractarianism to Ritualism: A Study of Some Aspects of Tractarianism Outside Oxford, From the Time of Newman's Conversion in 1845, Until the First Ritual Commission in 1867" (D. Phil. thesis, University of Oxford, 1984).

74. Chadwick, *Spirit of the Oxford Movement,* 49.

75. Palmer, *Narrative of Events,* 36–37.

76. Newman's Anglican sermons have been republished recently. *John Henry*

Newman: Sermons, 1824–1843, 2 vols., vol. 1, ed. Placid Murray, vol. 2, ed. Vincent Ferrer Blehl (Oxford: Clarendon Press, 1991, 1993).

77. Palmer, *Narrative of Events*, 35.

78. For a recent exposition of the Arian heresy, see Khalad Anatolios, *Athanasius: The Coherence of His Thought* (London: Routledge, 1998).

79. J. H. Newman, *The Arians of the Fourth Century* (London: Longmans, Green, 1890), 373.

80. This and other features of the Tractarian encounter with patristic theology are expounded in Nicolas Lossky, "The Oxford Movement and the Revival of Patristic Theology," in Vaiss, *From Oxford to the People*, 76–82.

81. Ibid., 79.

82. Newman, *Apologia*, 37.

83. Newman, *Arians*, 72.

84. Ibid., 137.

85. Newman, *Apologia*, 35.

86. J. H. Newman, *The Letters and Diaries of John Henry Newman*, vol. 30, ed. C. S. Dessain (Oxford: Clarendon Press, 1983), 105, 240.

87. Newman, *Apologia*, 36.

88. Gabriel O'Donnell, "The Spirituality of E. B. Pusey," in *Pusey Rediscovered*, ed. Perry Butler (London: SPCK, 1983), 247.

89. Sheridan Gilley, *Newman and His Age* (London: Darton, Longman and Todd, 1990), 91.

90. Newman, *Apologia*, 60.

91. He was vicar of St. Mary's from 1828 to 1843.

92. *John Henry Newman: Sermons, 1824–1843*, 1:v.

93. Ibid., vi.

94. "Course on the Liturgy," reprinted in ibid., 55–113.

95. See Chapter 5.

96. *John Henry Newman: Sermons, 1824–1843*, 1:74.

97. Newman, *Apologia*, 274.

98. Ibid., 411.

99. [J. H. Newman], *Tracts for the Times*, no. 6, "The Present Obligation of Primitive Practice" (1833).

100. Ibid.

101. [J. H. Newman], *Tracts for the Times*, no. 15, "On the Apostolical Succession in the English Church" (1833).

102. Rune Imberg, *In Quest of Authority* (Lund: Lund University Press, 1987).

103. [J. H. Newman], *Tracts for the Times*, no. 41, "Via Media—No. II" (1834).

104. [J. H. Newman], *Tracts for the Times*, no.1, "Thoughts on the Ministerial Commission respectfully addressed to the Clergy by one of themselves" (1833).

105. Newman, *Apologia*, 56.

106. Ibid., 54–57.

107. [J. Keble], *Tracts for the Times*, no. 4, "Adherence to the Apostolical Succession the Safest Course" (1833).

108. Ibid.

109. [J. Keble], *Tracts for the Times,* no. 89, "On the Mysticism attributed to the Early Fathers of the Church" (1841).

110. Battiscombe, *John Keble,* 229.

111. [E. B. Pusey], *Tracts for the Times,* no. 18, "Thoughts on the Benefits of the System of Fasting Enjoined by our Church" (1834).

112. [E. B. Pusey], *Tracts for the Times,* no. 68, "Scriptural Views of Holy Baptism" (1835).

113. Ibid.

114. Robert Harvie Greenfield, "'Such a Friend to the Pope,'" in Butler, *Pusey Rediscovered,* 162.

115. Newman, *Apologia,* 66.

116. *John Henry Newman: Autobiographical Writings,* ed. Henry Tristam (New York: Garland, 1957), 203.

117. Quoted in Battiscombe, *John Keble,* 292.

118. J. H. Newman, *Lectures on the Doctrine of Justification,* 2d ed. (London: Rivington, 1840), v.

119. Ibid., 326.

120. Ibid., 138.

121. Ibid., 154.

122. Ibid., 332–37.

123. Quoted in *John Henry Newman: Autobiographical Writings,* 77.

124. A piece of doggerel made the rounds: "There is not a rubber, where *outcast Jubber,* Is not thought an injur'd Woman, There's not a party, Where young Men Hearty, Would not horsewhip Mr Newman." Quoted in Gilley, *Newman and His Age,* 129.

125. *The Letters and Diaries of John Henry Newman,* vol. 4, ed. Ian Ker and Thomas Gornall (Oxford: Clarendon Press, 1980), 295.

126. Ibid., 293.

127. For an elaboration of the evangelicals and the Oxford Movement, see Peter Toon, *Evangelical Theology, 1833–1856: A Response to Tractarianism* (London: Marshall, Morgan and Scott, 1979).

128. William Goode, *The Divine Rule of Faith,* vol. 1 (London: Rivington, 1842), 36.

129. Pusey-Shaftesbury correspondence, May 17–July 27, 1852, Pusey MSS, Pusey House, Oxford.

130. See W.S.F. Pickering, *Anglo-Catholicism: A Study in Religious Ambiguity* (London: Mowbray, 1989), and J. Bentley, *Ritualism and Politics in Victorian England: The Attempt to Legislate for Belief* (Oxford: Clarendon Press, 1978).

Chapter 3

1. See Geoffrey Faber, *Oxford Apostles: A Character Study of the Oxford Movement,* 2d ed. (London: Faber and Faber, 1974).

2. J. H. Newman to Samuel Rickards, [March 1, 1836], in *The Letters and Diaries*

of John Henry Newman, vol. 5, ed. Thomas Gornall (Oxford: Clarendon Press, 1981), 247.

3. Georgina Battiscombe, *John Keble: A Study in Limitations* (London: Constable, 1963), 13.

4. Ibid., 18.

5. Thomas Mozley, *Reminiscences Chiefly of Oriel College and the Oxford Movement* (Cambridge: Riverside Press, 1882), 1:219.

6. Quoted in Battiscombe, *John Keble,* 47.

7. *The Letters and Diaries of John Henry Newman,* vol. 22, ed. Charles Stephen Dessain (London: Thomas Nelson and Sons, 1961), 209.

8. Quoted in Piers Brendon, *Hurrell Froude and the Oxford Movement* (London: Paul Elek, 1974), 8.

9. Quoted in Battiscombe, *John Keble,* 73.

10. Quoted in Sheridan Gilley, *Newman and His Age* (London: Darton, Longman and Todd, 1990), 42.

11. Geoffrey Faber, *Oxford Apostles: A Character Study of the Oxford Movement* (London: Faber and Faber, 1933).

12. Faber, *Oxford Apostles,* 2d ed., 223–25.

13. Quoted in Meriol Trevor, *Newman: The Pillar of the Cloud* (London: Macmillan, 1962), 90.

14. Brendon, *Hurrell Froude,* 74; *Remains of the Late Richard Hurrell Froude, M.A.,* 2 vols., ed. J. H. Newman and John Keble (London: Rivington, 1838–39).

15. J. H. Newman, *Apologia Pro Vita Sua,* ed. Martin J. Svaglic (Oxford: Clarendon Press, 1967), 47.

16. "Marriage is a very second rate business," Newman decided. Quoted in Newman, *The Via Media* (London: Longmans, Green, 1841), 2:154. Marrying, Froude believed, would be "to rat," to sell out to Protestant conventionality. Froude, *Remains,* 1:385.

17. Brendon, *Hurrell Froude,* 75.

18. Rodney Stenning Edgecombe, *Two Poets of the Oxford Movement: John Keble and John Henry Newman* (London: Associated University Press, 1996), chaps. 2 and 3.

19. Quoted in Battiscombe, *John Keble,* 104.

20. Quoted in *The Letters and Correspondence of John Henry Newman During His Life in the English Church,* ed. Anne Mozley (Oxford: Oxford University Press, 1891), 1:153.

21. John Keble to E. B. Pusey, October 2, 1827, Pusey MSS, Pusey House, Oxford.

22. Newman, *Letters and Correspondence,* 1:202.

23. J. H. Newman to Charles Portales Golightly, June 10, 1832, in *The Letters and Diaries of John Henry Newman,* vol. 2, ed. Ian Ker and Thomas Gornall (Oxford: Clarendon Press, 1979), 55.

24. Brendon, *Hurrell Froude,* 112.

25. Quoted in Battiscombe, *John Keble,* 131.

26. J. H. Newman to Henry Wilberforce, July 16, 1833, in Newman, *Letters and Diaries,* 2:9.

27. Brendon, *Hurrell Froude,* 113.

28. Froude, *Remains,* 1:282.

29. J. H. Newman to Harriett Newman, January 2, 1833, in *The Letters and Diaries of John Henry Newman,* vol. 3, ed. Ian Ker and Thomas Gornall (Oxford: Clarendon Press, 1979), 181.

30. J. H. Newman to Harriett Newman, February 16, 1833, in Newman, *Letters and Diaries,* 3:211.

31. J. H. Newman to Frederic Rogers, March 5, 1833, in Newman, *Letters and Diaries,* 3:234.

32. Brendon, *Hurrell Froude,* 113.

33. J. H. Newman to Henry Jenkyns, April 7, 1833, in Newman, *Letters and Diaries,* 3:280.

34. Froude, *Remains,* 1:434.

35. Newman, *Apologia,* 43.

36. Marvin O'Connell, "Newman and Lamennais," in *Newman After a Hundred Years,* ed. Ian Ker and Alan G. Hill (Oxford: Clarendon Press, 1990), 182.

37. *The Autobiography of Isaac Williams,* ed. George Prevost (London: Longmans, Green, 1892), 64.

38. Newman, *Apologia,* 43.

39. Gilley, *Newman and His Age,* 113.

40. See, for example, J. H. Newman to H. A. Woodgate, April 17, 1833, in Newman, *Letters and Diaries,* 3:297.

41. Robin Sharwood, "The Oriel Common Room of 1833," in *Colonial Tractarians: The Oxford Movement in Australia,* ed. Brian Porter (Melbourne: Joint Board of Christian Education, 1989), 148.

42. According to the 1834 university calendar (corrected to December 31, 1833), Oriel College had fifteen fellows besides Newman, Froude, and Keble. *Oxford University Calendar 1834,* 182–83.

43. Sharwood, "Oriel Common Room," 151.

44. H.C.G. Matthew, "Edward Bouverie Pusey: From Scholar to Tractarian," *Journal of Theological Studies* 32 (1981): 110.

45. Newman, *Apologia,* 15.

46. J. H. Newman to Simeon Lloyd Pope, March 3, 1836, in *The Letters and Diaries of John Henry Newman,* vol. 5, ed. Gerard Tracey (Oxford: Clarendon Press, 1995), 251.

47. Froude, *Remains,* 1:vi.

48. Ibid., xiv.

49. Ibid., 30.

50. Ibid., 252.

51. Ibid., 389.

52. Ibid., 435.

53. Ibid., 437.

54. Ibid., 434.

55. J. H. Newman to John Bowden, [January 17, 1838], in *The Letters and Diaries of John Henry Newman,* vol. 6, ed. Gerard Tracey (Oxford: Clarendon Press, 1984), 188.

56. "No don," writes Noel Annan convincingly, "has ever captivated Oxford as John Henry Newman did." Noel Annan, *The Dons: Mentors, Eccentrics and Geniuses* (London: HarperCollins, 1999), 41.

57. Matthew Arnold, *Philistinism in England and America* (Ann Arbor: University of Michigan Press, 1974), 165.

58. Newman, *Apologia*, 76.

59. Pusey and Blomfield had a wide correspondence on this and other topics, which can be read in "Bishop Blomfield to E. B. Pusey, 1830–1855," Pusey MSS, Pusey House, Oxford.

60. Thomas Arnold, "The Oxford Malignants and Dr Hampden," *The Edinburgh Review* 63 (April 1836): 237–39.

61. Newman, *Apologia*, 91.

62. J. H. Newman to Mrs. John Mozley (Jemima Newman), April 23, 1839, in Newman, *Letters and Diaries*, 6:66–67.

63. The memorial still stands in Magdalen Street.

64. Newman, *Apologia*, 111.

65. Newman, *Letters and Correspondence*, 2:286.

66. Ibid.

67. Battiscombe, *John Keble*, 217.

68. [J. H. Newman], *Tracts for the Times*, no. 90, "On Certain Passages in the XXXIX Articles" (1841), 5.

69. J. H. Newman to E. B. Pusey, March 10, 1841, Pusey MSS, Pusey House, Oxford.

70. Quoted in Ian Ker, *John Henry Newman: A Biography* (Oxford: Oxford University Press, 1988), 219.

71. *Correspondence of John Henry Newman with John Keble and Others, 1839–1845*, [ed. Joseph Bacchus] (London: Longmans, Green, 1917), 210–11.

72. David Newsome probes the theme in *The Parting of Friends: A Study of the Wilberforces and the Mannings* (Cambridge: Harvard University Press, Belknap Press, 1966).

73. Gilley, *Newman and His Age*, 220.

74. W. G. Ward, *The Ideal of a Christian Church Considered in Comparison with Existing Practice* (London: James Toovey, 1844), 241.

75. E. B. Pusey to John Keble, March 28, 1845, Pusey MSS (copies), Pusey House, Oxford.

76. Quoted in Ker, *John Henry Newman*, 301.

77. John Keble to E. B. Pusey, October 21, 1845, Pusey MSS (copies), Pusey House, Oxford.

78. Quoted in Battiscombe, *John Keble*, 262.

79. J. H. Newman to John Keble, November 14, 1845, *The Letters and Diaries of John Henry Newman*, vol. 11, ed. Charles Stephen Dessain (London: Thomas Nelson and Sons, 1961), 34.

80. J. H. Newman to E. B. Pusey, October 8, 1845, in Newman, *Letters and Diaries*, 11:8.

81. T. Mozley, *Reminiscences of Oriel College*, 1:448.

82. R. W. Church, *The Oxford Movement: Twelve Years, 1833–1845,* ed. Geoffrey Best (Chicago: University of Chicago Press, 1970), 260. However, Marriott was unswerving in his loyalty to Oxford. In high dudgeon, he put it this way in 1845: "For my own part though I may be suspected, hampered, worried, and perhaps actually persecuted, I will fight every inch of ground before I will be compelled to forsake the services of that mother to whom I know new birth in Christ, and the milk of His word. I will not forsake her at any man's bidding." *Dictionary of National Biography* (London: Oxford University Press, 1937), 9:1082.

83. See Herbert Paul, *The Life of Froude,* 2d ed. (London: Pitman, 1906).

84. Tractarians abroad are addressed in Chapter 5.

85. For example, All Saints, Margaret Street.

86. The extensive correspondence between Pusey and Hook in the late 1840s is by turns unintentionally comic and deadly serious. It epitomizes well the Catholic-Protestant tensions extant in the Church of England and the crux of Pusey's ongoing dilemma. "E. B. Pusey to W.F. Hook (1827–1848)," Pusey MSS (copies), Pusey House, Oxford. See also Nigel Yates, "The Oxford Movement and Parish Life: St. Saviour's, Leeds, 1839–1929" (University of York: Borthwick Papers, 1975).

87. Battiscombe, *John Keble,* 269. Her comment alludes to Froude's famous remark concerning Keble and Newman: "Do you know the story of the murderer who had done one good thing in his life? Well, if I was ever asked what good deed I have ever done, I should say I had brought Newman and Keble to understand each other." Froude, *Remains,* 1:438.

88. Newsome, *The Parting of Friends.*

89. Battiscombe, *John Keble,* 349.

90. As described by Newman in a letter to his mother on May 3, 1822, in *The Letters and Diaries of John Henry Newman,* vol. 1, ed. Ian Ker and Thomas Gornall (Oxford: Clarendon Press, 1978), 139.

Chapter 4

1. See G. Kitson Clark, *Churchmen and the Condition of England, 1832–1885* (London: Methuen, 1973).

2. Over the course of the first half of the nineteenth century the population of England and Wales doubled, from just under nine million to almost eighteen million. These figures come from G. Kitson Clark, *The Making of Victorian England* (London: Methuen, 1985), 66.

3. See Richard Allen Soloway, *Prelates and People: Ecclesiastical Social Thought in England, 1783–1852* (London: Routledge and Kegan Paul, 1969).

4. See Boyd Hilton, *The Age of Atonement: The Influence of Evangelicalism on Social and Economic Thought, 1795–1865* (Oxford: Clarendon Press, 1988), chap. 2.

5. Soloway, *Prelates and People,* 160.

6. See Peter Mandler, "Tories and Paupers: Christian Political Economy and the Making of the New Poor Law," *The Historical Journal* 33, no. 1 (1990): 81–103.

7. Ibid., 81.

8. Hilton, *Age of Atonement,* chap. 6.

9. Richard Whately, *Introductory Lectures on Political Economy,* 2d ed. (London: Fellowes, 1832), vii.

10. William George Peck, *The Social Implications of the Oxford Movement* (New York: Scribner's, 1934), 44.

11. J. H. Newman to Richard Whately, October 28, 1834, in *The Letters and Diaries of John Henry Newman,* vol. 4, ed. Ian Ker and Thomas Gornall (Oxford: Clarendon Press, 1980), 349.

12. J. H. Newman, *Apologia Pro Vita Sua,* ed. Martin J. Svaglic (Oxford: Clarendon Press, 1967), 12.

13. Richard Whately, *The Kingdom of Christ* (London: J. Murray, 1841), 44.

14. Whately, *Introductory Lectures,* 103.

15. Soloway, *Prelates and People,* 182.

16. See Maurice B. Reckitt, *From Maurice to Temple* (London: SPCK, 1947), 35.

17. Terence Kenny, *The Political Thought of John Henry Newman* (London: Longmans, Green, 1957), 172. See, also, Edward Norman, "Newman's Social and Political Thinking," in *Newman After a Hundred Years,* ed. Ian Ker and Alan G. Hill (Oxford: Clarendon Press, 1990), 153–73.

18. C. S. Dessain, *John Henry Newman,* 2d ed. (London: Oxford University Press, 1971), 70.

19. [S. R. Bosanquet,] "Private Alms and Poor-law Relief," *British Critic* 28 (October 1840): 453.

20. Reckitt, *From Maurice to Temple,* 35.

21. K. S. Inglis, *Churches and the Working Classes in Victorian England* (London: Routledge and Kegan Paul, 1963), 251.

22. J.H.L. Rowlands, *Church, State and Society: The Attitudes of John Keble, Richard Hurrell Froude and John Henry Newman, 1827–1845* (Worthing, West Sussex: Churchman Publishing, 1989), 219.

23. See Violet M. Howse, *Pusey: A Parish Record* (Oxford: Holywell Press, 1972).

24. E. B. Pusey to Phillip Pusey, March 4, 1845, Pusey MSS, Pusey House, Oxford.

25. For their correspondence, see "Bishop Blomfield to E. B. Pusey, 1830–1855," Pusey MSS, Pusey House, Oxford.

26. See R. W. Franklin, *Nineteenth-Century Churches: The History of a New Catholicism in Wurttemberg, England, and France* (New York: Garland, 1987).

27. R. W. Franklin, "Pusey and Worship in Industrial Society," *Worship* 57, no. 5 (September 1983): 388.

28. Quoted in H. P. Liddon, *Life of Edward Bouverie Pusey* (London: Longmans, Green, 1893–97), 3:171.

29. See Nigel Yates, "The Oxford Movement and Parish Life: St. Saviour's, Leeds, 1839–1929" (University of York: Borthwick Institute, 1975).

30. Liddon, *Life of Pusey,* 3:86.

31. My comments here rely on the work of Sean Gill in *Women and the Church of England: From the Eighteenth Century to the Present* (London: SPCK, 1994), chap. 3.

32. Quoted in ibid., 81.

33. Liddon, *Life of Pusey,* 3:5.

34. Eighteen sisterhoods in some ninety-five centers were established by 1875. Brian Heeney, *The Women's Movement in the Church of England: 1850–1930* (Oxford: Clarendon Press, 1988), 63. See also Thomas Jay Williams and Allan Walter Campbell, *The Park Village Sisterhood* (London: SPCK, 1965).

35. Liddon, *Life of Pusey,* 3:2. Popular feeling could run extremely high, however. In 1850, when the Pusey-inspired Devonport sisterhood ceremonially marked its foundation, the assembled clergy and sisters endured a barrage of "potatoes and plates" thrown by some of the townspeople. Gill, *Women and the Church of England,* 151.

36. For a nuanced study of Anglican sisterhoods, see Susan Mumm, *Stolen Daughters, Virgin Mothers: Anglican Sisterhoods in Victorian Britain* (London: Leicester University Press, 1999) and, by the same author, *All Saints Sisters of the Poor: An Anglican Sisterhood in the Nineteenth Century* (Woodbridge: Boydell Press, 2001).

37. Bishop Blomfield to E. B. Pusey, June 4, 1855, Pusey MSS, Pusey House, Oxford.

38. See John Shelton Reed, "A 'Female Movement': The Feminization of Nineteenth-Century Anglo-Catholicism," *Anglican and Episcopal History* 57, no. 2 (June 1988): 199–238.

39. Mumm, *Stolen Daughters, Virgin Mothers,* 3–5.

40. A short distance, as it happened, from Park Village.

41. Georgina Battiscombe, *Christina Rossetti: A Divided Life* (London: Constable, 1981), 31.

42. W. M. Rossetti, *Some Reminiscences,* vol. 1 (London: Brown Langham, 1906), 1.

43. See Jan Marsh, *Christina Rossetti: A Literary Biography* (London: Jonathan Cape, 1994), 55–64.

44. William Rossetti quoted in ibid., 64.

45. Marsh, *Christina Rossetti,* 57.

46. Meaning, in the view of one of Yonge's biographers, "truthfulness, self-sacrifice, true courage, self-control, filial piety, the humility which scrutinizes and repents the smallest sin." Alethea Hayter, *Charlotte Yonge* (Plymouth: Northcote House, 1996), 18.

47. Barbara Dennis, *Charlotte Yonge (1823–1901): Novelist of the Oxford Movement* (Queenston, Ont.: The Edwin Mellen Press, 1992), 2.

48. Hayter, *Charlotte Yonge,* 21.

49. Quoted in ibid., 20.

50. See David B. McIlhiney, *A Gentleman in Every Slum: Church of England Missions in East London, 1837–1914* (Allison Park, Pa.: Pickwick Publications, 1988), chap. 2.

51. E. B. Pusey to J. H. Newman, January 11, 1837, Pusey MSS, Pusey House, Oxford.

52. J. H. Newman, *Parochial and Plain Sermons,* vol. 5 (London: Rivington, 1840), dedicatory page.

53. E. B. Pusey to Henry Manning, April 17, 1837, Pusey MSS, Pusey House, Oxford.

54. ACS *Reports* (1838), Additional Curates Society Archives, Birmingham.

55. *Minute Book No. 1,* Additional Curates Society Archives, Birmingham.

56. ACS *Reports* (1838), Additional Curates Society Archives, Birmingham.

57. E. B. Pusey to J. H. Newman, September 18, 1839, Pusey MSS, Pusey House, Oxford.

58. E. B. Pusey to Joshua Watson, October 30, 1839, Keble MSS, Keble College, Oxford.

59. Edward Churton to Joshua Watson, September 7, 1842, Churton MSS, Pusey House, Oxford.

60. Edward Churton to Joshua Watson, February 6, 1843, Churton MSS, Pusey House, Oxford.

61. Joshua Watson, "Reminiscences," ed. Mary Watson, appendix, Additional Curates Society Archives, Birmingham.

62. *Minute Book No. 2,* Additional Curates Society Archives, Birmingham.

63. ACS *Home Mission Field* (1861), Additional Curates Society Archives, Birmingham.

64. A notable recent exception is George William Herring, *Tractarianism to Ritualism: A Study of Some Aspects of Tractarianism Outside Oxford, From the Time of Newman's Conversion in 1845,Until the First Ritual Commission in 1867* (D. Phil. thesis, University of Oxford, 1984).

65. Augustus W.N. Pugin, *Contrasts: Or, a Parallel between the Noble Edifices of the Middle Ages, and Corresponding Buildings of the Present Day; Shewing the Present Decay of Taste* (London: Dolman, 1841). A somewhat different edition had come out in 1836.

66. Thomas Rickman, *An Attempt to Discriminate the Styles of Architecture in England, from the Conquest to the Reformation* (London: Dolman, 1817), and M. H. Bloxam, *The Principles of Gothic Ecclesiastical Architecture* (London: George Bell, 1829).

67. These statistics come from James Stevens Curl, *Victorian Churches* (London: B. T. Batsford, 1995), 50. See, also, Colin Cunningham, *Stones of Witness: Church Architecture and Function* (Stroud, Gloucestershire: Sutton, 1999).

68. Curl, *Victorian Churches,* 50.

69. See Owen Chadwick, *The Secularization of the European Mind in the Nineteenth Century* (Cambridge: Cambridge University Press, 1990).

70. Roy Jenkins, *Gladstone* (London: Macmillan, 1995).

71. See, for example, M. J. Lynch, "Was Gladstone a Tractarian? W. E. Gladstone and the Oxford Movement, 1833–45," *Journal of Religious History* 13 (1975): 364–89.

72. W. E. Gladstone to A.W. Hutton, April 21, 1892, British Library Additional MS 44215, f. 256.

73. E. J. Feuchtwanger, *Gladstone,* 2d ed. (Basingstoke: Macmillan, 1989), 14.

74. W. E. Gladstone, *The State in Its Relations with the Church,* 4th ed. (London: J. Murray, 1841), 1:77–78.

75. Ibid., 4.

76. W. E. Gladstone, *Church Principles Considered in their Results* (London: J. Murray, 1840), 374.

77. See Perry Butler, *Gladstone Church, State, and Tractarianism: A Study of His Religious Ideas and Attitudes* (Oxford: Clarendon Press, 1982).

78. Richard J. Helmstadter, "Conscience and Politics: Gladstone's First Book," in *The Gladstonian Turn of Mind*, ed. Bruce L. Kinzer (Toronto: University of Toronto Press, 1985), 35.

79. *The Gladstone Diaries*, ed. M.R.D. Foot and H.C.G. Matthew, vol. 3 (Oxford: Clarendon Press, 1974), May 9, 1841.

80. W. E. Gladstone to J. H. Newman, September 19, 1844, Newman MSS, The Oratory, Birmingham.

81. David W. Bebbington, *William Ewart Gladstone: Faith and Politics in Victorian Britain* (Grand Rapids, Mich.: Eerdmans, 1993), 62.

82. *British Critic* 26 (October 1839).

83. Ibid., 367.

84. Butler, *Gladstone Church, State, and Tractarianism*, 89.

85. See H.C.G. Matthew, *Gladstone, 1809–1874* (Oxford: Clarendon Press, 1986), 90–95, and *Gladstone Diaries*, 3:435–36. See, also by Matthew, "Gladstone, Evangelicalism and 'The Engagement,'" in *Revival and Religion Since 1700: Essays for John Walsh*, ed. Jane Garnett and Colin Matthew (Rio Grande, Ohio: Hambledon, 1993), 111–26.

86. *Gladstone Diaries*, 9:240.

87. Quoted in Bebbington, *William Ewart Gladstone*, 199.

88. Ibid., 183.

89. Robert Blake, *Disraeli* (New York: St. Martin's Press, 1967), 550.

90. Quoted in ibid.

91. Ibid., 551.

92. H.C.G. Matthew, *Gladstone 1875–1898* (Oxford: Clarendon Press, 1994), 391.

Chapter 5

1. John D. Davies, *The Faith Abroad* (Oxford: Basil Blackwell, 1983), 47.

2. Stephen Neill, *A History of Christian Missions*, 2d ed. (Markham, Ont.: Penguin, 1987), 215.

3. See Eyre Chatterton, *A History of the Church of England in India* (London: SPCK, 1924), and George Smith, *Henry Martyn* (New York: F. H. Revell, 1892). The Oxford Mission to India, which was founded in 1880 and emanated from the Anglo-Catholics at Oxford, invoked the spirit of Henry Martyn. R. M. Benson himself, however, founder of the Cowley Fathers and guiding light of the Mission, looked much more closely to Pusey for inspiration. See *A Hundred Years in Bengal: A History of the Oxford Mission, 1880–1980. By Two of the Brethren of the Epiphany* (Delhi: ISPCK, 1979).

4. See Mark A. Noll, *A History of Christianity in the United States and Canada* (Grand Rapids, Mich.: Eerdmans, 1993).

5. See Eugene Stock, *History of the Church Missionary Society*, 4 vols. (London: Church Missionary Society, 1899–1916), and H. P. Thompson, *Into All Lands: The*

History of the Society for the Propagation of the Gospel in Foreign Parts, 1701–1900 (London: SPCK, 1951).

6. See Linda Colley, *Britons: Forging the Nation, 1707–1832* (New Haven: Yale University Press, 1992). As well, David Cannadine, *Ornamentalism: How the British Saw Their Empire* (Oxford: Oxford University Press, 2001).

7. Newman recorded his visit on July 3 in this self-deprecating way: "They say weakness of voice, shortness of sight, want of eloquence, are not sufficient impediments. Indeed the Stations most deficiently filled are such as, requiring scholastic attainments, do not require bodily vigour etc." Quoted in *The Letters and Diaries of John Henry Newman,* vol. 1, ed. Ian Ker and Thomas Gornall (Oxford: Clarendon Press, 1978), 177.

8. J. H. Newman, *The Via Media* (London: Longmans, Green, 1841), 2:3.

9. Tom Mozley wrote of his future brother-in-law Newman's dealings with the Church Missionary Society to his sister Anne Mozley in an informative and prophetic letter: "Newman . . . has been completely discomfited in the matter of the Missionary Society. . . . [L]ast Monday when there was a general meeting to elect officers, when they generally re-elect the old ones and just fill up the vacancies, he was ousted by an immense majority. . . . He has, to be sure, given the Low Church party great provocation. . . . [B]ut Newman is not a man to be deterred by temporary failures. He is, indeed, better calculated than any man I know, by his talents, his learning, by his patience and perseverance, his conciliatory *manners,* and the friends he can employ in the cause—of whom I hope to be one—to release the Church of England from her present oppressed and curtailed condition." Tom Mozley to Anne Mozley, March 14, 1830, in *The Letters and Diaries of John Henry Newman,* vol. 2, ed. Ian Ker and Thomas Gornall (Oxford: Clarendon Press, 1979), 199.

10. Newman, *Via Media,* 2:15.

11. Just fourteen students, by Froude's count. Richard Hurrell Froude, *Hurrell Froude: Memoranda and Comments,* ed. Louise Imogen Guiney (London: Methuen, 1904), 150.

12. Quoted in ibid.

13. *Remains of the Late Reverend Richard Hurrell Froude, M.A.,* 2 vols., ed. J. H. Newman and John Keble (London: Rivington, 1838), 1:377.

14. Froude, *Hurrell Froude,* 139.

15. Ibid., 132.

16. Froude, *Remains,* 1:400–401.

17. Ibid., 380.

18. David Forrester, *Young Doctor Pusey* (London: SPCK, 1989), 185.

19. E. B. Pusey, "The Church the Converter of the Heathen," in *Parochial Sermons Preached and Printed on Various Occasions,* vols. 11 and 12 (Oxford: John Henry Parker, 1865).

20. Ibid., 11:11; 12:29, 39.

21. Ibid., 12:47.

22. Bishop Blomfield to E. B. Pusey, June 2 and November 4 and 7, 1840, and April 3 and 21, 1841; E. B. Pusey to Archdeacon Benjamin Harrison (MSS copies), July 6 and 20 and September 3, 1838, and October 18, 1839, Pusey MSS, Pusey House, Oxford.

23. For a fuller account of Pusey's position on missions, see Ruth Teale, "Dr Pusey and the Church Overseas," in *Pusey Rediscovered,* ed. Perry Butler (London: SPCK, 1983), 185–209.

24. These famous words of Livingstone's form part of the inscription on his tomb at Westminster Abbey, London.

25. David Livingstone, *Dr Livingstone's Cambridge Lectures,* ed. W. Monk (Cambridge: Deighton, Bell, 1860), 12.

26. See Tim Jeal, *Livingstone* (Markham, Ont.: Penguin, 1985); Reginald Coupland, *Kirk on the Zambesi* (Oxford: Clarendon Press, 1968); Owen Chadwick, *Mackenzie's Grave* (London: Hodder and Stoughton, 1959). Also, Brad Faught, "Tractarianism on the Zambesi: Bishop Mackenzie and the Beginnings of the Universities Mission to Central Africa," *Anglican and Episcopal History* 66, no. 3 (September 1997): 303–28.

27. Chadwick, *Mackenzie's Grave,* 22.

28. *Appeal to the Members of the University of Oxford on Behalf of the Oxford and Cambridge Mission to Central Africa,* Occasional Paper, 1859.

29. Quoted in Charles Gray, *Life of Robert Gray, Bishop of Cape Town and Metropolitan of Africa,* vol. 1 (London: Rivington, 1876), 440.

30. Bishop Gray to E. B. Pusey, March 28, 1859, Pusey MSS, Pusey House, Oxford.

31. Charles F. Mackenzie to Bishop Wilberforce, February 13, 1860, f. 9, MS. Wilberforce c. 19, Bodleian Library, Oxford.

32. Quoted in Chadwick, *Mackenzie's Grave,* 192.

33. Mackenzie's was not the only death in the founding period of the UMCA. His partner in the journey to the confluence of the Shire and Ruo rivers, Henry Burrup, died a few days after stumbling back into Magomero bearing news of the bishop's death. Two more UMCA missionaries, Henry Scudamore and John Dickinson, died in 1863.

34. See, for example, William Westfall, *Two Worlds: The Protestant Culture of Nineteenth-Century Ontario* (Montreal and Kingston: McGill-Queen's University Press, 1989), and John Webster Grant, *A Profusion of Spires: Religion in Nineteenth-Century Ontario* (Toronto: University of Toronto Press, 1988).

35. See David Flint, *John Strachan: Pastor and Politician* (Toronto: Oxford University Press, 1971).

36. See Lawrence Shook, "Newman's Correspondence with two Canadians," *Dublin Review* 234 (Autumn 1960): 205–21.

37. Strachan's correspondence with Newman can be found in *The Letters and Diaries of John Henry Newman,* vol. 7, ed. Gerard Tracey (Oxford: Clarendon Press, 1995), 122, 144, 154–55, 163–64, 166.

38. John Kenyon, "The Influence of the Oxford Movement upon the Church of England in Upper Canada," *Ontario History* 51, no. 2, (1959): 82.

39. John Strachan to Henry Patton, 19 November 1845, in Strachan Letter Book," Archives of Ontario, Toronto.

40. Quoted in Piers Brendon, *Hurrell Froude and the Oxford Movement* (London: Paul Elek, 1974), 120.

41. Grant, *A Profusion of Spires,* 128.

42. See Brad Faught, "John Charles Roper and the Oxford Movement in To-

ronto," *Journal of the Canadian Church Historical Society* 36, no. 2 (October 1994): 113–33.

43. The biographical information on Broughton comes from G. P. Shaw, *Patriarch and Patriot: William Grant Broughton 1788–1853* (Melbourne: Melbourne University Press, 1978).

44. Quoted in Austin Cooper, "Bishop Broughton and the Diocese of Australia," in *Colonial Tractarians: The Oxford Movement in Australia,* ed. Brian Porter (Melbourne: Joint Board of Christian Education, 1989), 30.

45. Quoted in Teale, "Dr. Pusey and the Church Overseas," 198.

46. For a detailed elaboration of the Colenso case, see G. W. Cox, *Life of Bishop Colenso,* 2 vols. (London: Ridgeway, 1888). Also, Gray, *Life of Robert Gray,* and G. Parsons, "Rethinking the Missionary Position: Bishop Colenso of Natal," in *Religion in Victorian Britain: Volume V, Culture and Empire,* ed. John Wolffe (Manchester: Manchester University Press, 1997), 135–75.

47. Quoted in Gray, *Life of Robert Gray,* 2:121.

48. Frances Knight, *The Nineteenth-Century Church and English Society* (Cambridge: Cambridge University Press, 1995), 1.

49. Quoted in H. P. Liddon, *Life of Edward Bouverie Pusey* (London: Longmans, Green, 1893–97), 3:346.

50. Teale, "Dr. Pusey and the Church Overseas," 202.

51. Disappointment and occasional bitterness at being sent to the colonies were apparent in many new ordinands. Notably, Featherstone Osler, father of Sir William Osler, the great Canadian physician and Regius Professor of Medicine at Oxford from 1905 to 1919, was one such cleric. However, eventually he grew to love his backwoods parish in the 1840s and 1850s, which at that time was on the Upper Canadian frontier northwest of Toronto. See Michael Bliss, *William Osler: A Life in Medicine* (Toronto: University of Toronto Press, 1999).

52. The first overseas diocese of the Church of England was created in loyalist Nova Scotia in 1787. See Peter M. Doll, "American High Churchmanship and the Establishment of the First Colonial Episcopate in the Church of England: Nova Scotia, 1787," *The Journal of Ecclesiastical History* 43, no. 1 (January 1992): 35–59.

53. For elaboration on the period, see John F. Woolverton, *Colonial Anglicanism in North America* (Detroit: Wayne State University Press, 1984), and Raymond W. Albright, *A History of the Protestant Episcopal Church* (New York: Macmillan, 1964).

54. For a fuller reading of the stridency with which the Tractarians were attacked, see Charles P. McIlvaine, *The Chief Danger of the Church in These Times* (New York: Garland, 1843).

55. Quoted in E. Clowes Chorley, *Men and Movements in the American Episcopal Church* (New York: Scribner's, 1946), 208–9.

56. *Proceedings and Debates of the General Convention of 1844,* 95

57. R. William Franklin has done considerable work on Pusey's view of the Eucharist. See, for example, "Pusey and Worship in Industrial Society," *Worship* 57, no. 5 (September 1983): 386–412.

58. See Esther De Waal, "John Henry Hobart and the Early Oxford Movement," *Anglican Theological Review* 65, no. 3 (July 1983): 324–31.

59. Pusey, "The Church the Converter of the Heathen," in *Parochial Sermons,* 11:10.

Afterword

1. Adrian Hastings, *A History of Anglo-Catholicism, 1920–1985* (London: Collins, 1986), 174–75.

2. See Paul T. Phillips, *A Kingdom on Earth: Anglo-American Social Christianity, 1880–1940* (University Park: Pennsylvania State University Press, 1996).

Bibliography

Primary Sources

Additional Curates Society Archives, Birmingham.
Churton MSS, Pusey House, Oxford.
Gladstone Papers, British Library, Add. MSS 44086–44835.
Keble MSS, Keble College, Oxford.
Newman MSS, The Oratory, Birmingham.
Pusey MSS, Pusey House, Oxford.
"Strachan Letter Book," Archives of Ontario, Toronto.
Wilberforce MSS, Bodleian Library, Oxford.

Printed Primary Sources

Appeal to the Members of the University of Oxford on Behalf of the Oxford and Cambridge Mission to Central Africa. Occasional Paper, 1859.
British Critic.
Correspondence of John Henry Newman with John Keble and Others 1839–1845. [Ed. Joseph Bacchus.] London: Longmans, Green, 1917.
Dictionary of National Biography.
Froude, Richard Hurrell. *Hurrell Froude: Memoranda and Comments.* Ed. Louise Imogen Guiney. London: Methuen, 1904.
———. *Remains of the Late Richard Hurrell Froude, M.A.* 2 vols. Ed. J. H. Newman and John Keble. London: Rivington, 1838–39.
Keble, John. *The Christian Year.* London: Oxford University Press, 1914.
Gladstone, W. E. *Church Principles Considered in Their Results.* London: J. Murray, 1840.
———. *The Gladstone Diaries.* 14 vols. Ed. M.R.D. Foot and H.C.G. Matthew. Oxford: Clarendon Press, 1968–94.
———. *The State in Its Relations with the Church.* 4th ed. 2 vols. London: J. Murray, 1841.
———. *National Apostasy.* Introduction by Alan M.G. Stephenson. Abingdon, Oxfordshire, 1983.
Livingstone, David. *Dr Livingstone's Cambridge Lectures.* Ed. W. Monk. Cambridge: Deighton, Bell, 1860.

Mozley, Thomas. *Reminiscences Chiefly of Oriel College and the Oxford Movement.* 2 vols. Cambridge: Riverside Press, 1882.

Newman, John Henry. *Apologia Pro Vita Sua.* Ed. Martin J. Svaglic. Oxford: Clarendon Press, 1967.

———. *The Arians of the Fourth Century.* London: Longmans, Green, 1890.

———. *Discussions and Arguments on Various Subjects.* London: Rivington, 1873.

———. *John Henry Newman: Autobiographical Writings.* Ed. Henry Tristram. London: Macmillan, 1956; New York: Garland, 1957.

———. *John Henry Newman: Sermons, 1824–184.* 2 vols. Vol. 1, ed. Placid Murray. Vol. 2, ed. Vincent Ferrer Blehl. Oxford: Clarendon Press, 1991, 1993.

———. *Lectures on the Doctrine of Justification.* 2d ed. London: Rivington, 1840.

———. *The Letters and Correspondence of John Henry Newman During His Life in the English Church.* 2 vols. Ed. Anne Mozley. Oxford: Oxford University Press, 1891.

———. *The Letters and Diaries of John Henry Newman.* Vols. 1–31. Ed. C. S. Dessain et al. London: Thomas Nelson and Sons, 1961–72; Oxford: Clarendon Press, 1973–95.

———. *Parochial and Plain Sermons.* Vol. 5. London: Rivington, 1840.

———. *The Via Media.* 2 vols. London: Longmans, Green, 1841.

Oxford University Calendar 1834.

Proceedings and Debates of the General Convention of 1844. [Episcopal Church of the United States.]

Pusey, E. B. *Parochial Sermons Preached and Printed on Various Occasions.* Vols. 11 and 12. Oxford: John Henry Parker, 1865.

———. *The Royal Supremacy not an Arbitrary Authority But Limited by the Laws of the Church, of which Kings Are Members.* Oxford: John Henry Parker, 1850.

Rossetti, W. M. *Some Reminiscences.* Vol. 1. London: Brown Langham, 1906.

Tracts for the Times.

Williams, Isaac. *The Autobiography of Isaac Williams.* Ed. George Prevost. London: Longmans, Green, 1892.

Secondary Sources

Albright, Raymond W. *A History of the Protestant Episcopal Church.* New York: Macmillan, 1964.

Annan, Noel. *The Dons: Mentors, Eccentrics and Geniuses.* London: HarperCollins, 1999.

Anatolios, Khalad. *Athanasius: The Coherence of His Thought.* London: Routledge, 1998.

Arnold, Matthew. *Philistinism in England and America.* Ann Arbor: University of Michigan Press, 1974.

Battiscombe, Georgina. *Christina Rossetti: A Divided Life.* London: Constable, 1981.

————. *John Keble: A Study in Limitations.* London: Constable, 1963.

Bebbington, David W. *William Ewart Gladstone: Faith and Politics in Victorian Britain.* Grand Rapids, Mich.: Eerdmans, 1993.

Bentley, J. *Ritualism and Politics in Victorian England: The Attempt to Legislate for Belief.* Oxford: Clarendon Press, 1978.

Blake, Robert. *Disraeli.* New York: St. Martin's Press, 1967.

Bliss, Michael. *William Osler: A Life in Medicine.* Toronto: University of Toronto Press, 1999.

Bloxam, M. H. *The Principles of Gothic Ecclesiastical Architecture.* London: George Bell, 1829.

Bradford, Sarah. *Disraeli.* New York: Stein and Day, 1983.

Brendon, Piers. *Hurrell Froude and the Oxford Movement.* London: Paul Elek, 1974.

Brilioth, Yngve. *The Anglican Revival.* London: Longmans, Green, 1925.

Burns, Arthur. *The Diocesan Revival in the Church of England, c. 1800–1870.* Oxford: Clarendon Press, 1999.

Butler, Perry. *Gladstone Church, State, and Tractarianism: A Study of His Religious Ideas and Attitudes, 1809–1859.* Oxford: Clarendon Press, 1982.

————, ed. *Pusey Rediscovered.* London: SPCK, 1983.

Cannadine, David. *Ornamentalism: How the British Saw Their Empire.* Oxford: Oxford University Press, 2001.

Cecil, David. *Melbourne.* London: The Reprint Society, 1955.

Chadwick, Owen. *Mackenzie's Grave.* London: Hodder and Stoughton, 1959.

————. *The Secularization of the European Mind in the Nineteenth Century.* Cambridge: Cambridge University Press, 1990.

————. *The Spirit of the Oxford Movement: Tractarian Essays.* Cambridge: Cambridge University Press, 1990.

Chatterton, Eyre. *A History of the Church of England in India.* London: SPCK, 1924.

Chorley, E. Clowes. *Men and Movements in the American Episcopal Church.* New York: Scribner's, 1946.

Church, R. W. *The Oxford Movement: Twelve Years, 1833–1845.* London: Macmillan, 1891. Reprint edited by Geoffrey Best. Chicago: University of Chicago Press, 1970.

Clark, G. Kitson. *Churchmen and the Condition of England, 1832–1885.* London: Methuen, 1973.

————. *The Making of Victorian England.* London: Methuen, 1985.

Clark, J.C.D. *English Society, 1688–1832.* Cambridge: Cambridge University Press, 1985.

Colley, Linda. *Britons: Forging the Nation, 1707–1832.* New Haven: Yale University Press, 1992.

Coupland, Reginald. *Kirk on the Zambesi.* Oxford: Clarendon Press, 1968.

Cox, G. W. *Life of Bishop Colenso.* 2 vols. London: Ridgeway, 1888.

Crumb, Lawrence N. *The Oxford Movement and Its Leaders: A Bibliography of Sec-*

ondary and Lesser Primary Sources. Metuchen, N.J.: American Theological Library Association, Scarecrow Press, 1988. A supplement was published in 1993.

Curl, James Steven. *Victorian Churches.* London: B. T. Batsford, 1995.

Cunningham, Colin. *Stones of Witness: Church Architecture and Function.* Stroud, Gloucestershire: Sutton, 1999.

Davies, John D. *The Faith Abroad.* Oxford: Basil Blackwell, 1983.

Dennis, Barbara. *Charlotte Yonge (1823–1901): Novelist of the Oxford Movement.* Queenston, Ont.: The Edwin Mellen Press, 1992.

Dessain, C. S. *John Henry Newman.* 2d ed. London: Oxford University Press, 1971.

Edgecombe, Rodney Stenning. *Two Poets of the Oxford Movement: John Keble and John Henry Newman.* London: Associated University Press, 1996.

Faber, Geoffrey. *Oxford Apostles: A Character Study of the Oxford Movement.* 1st ed. London: Faber and Faber, 1933. 2d ed. London: Faber and Faber, 1974.

Feuchtwanger, E. J. *Gladstone.* 2d ed. Basingstoke: Macmillan, 1989.

Flint, David. *John Strachan: Pastor and Politician.* Toronto: Oxford University Press, 1971.

Forrester, David. *Young Doctor Pusey.* London: SPCK, 1989.

Franklin, R. W. *Nineteenth-Century Churches: The History of a New Catholicism in Wurttemberg, England, and France.* New York: Garland, 1987.

Garnett, Jane, and Colin Matthew. *Revival and Religion Since 1700: Essays for John Walsh.* Rio Grand, Ohio: Hambledon, 1993.

Gill, Sean. *Women and the Church of England: From the Eighteenth Century to the Present.* London: SPCK, 1994.

Gilley, Sheridan. *Newman and His Age.* London: Darton, Longman and Todd, 1990.

Goode, William. *The Divine Rule of Faith.* Vol. 1. London: Rivington, 1842.

Graham, Walter. *English Literary Periodicals.* New York: T. Nelson, 1930.

Grant, John Webster. *A Profusion of Spires: Religion in Nineteenth-Century Ontario.* Toronto: University of Toronto Press, 1988.

Gray, Charles. *Life of Robert Gray, Bishop of Cape Town and Metropolitan of Africa.* Vol. 1. London: Rivington, 1876.

Hastings, Adrian. *A History of Anglo-Catholicism, 1920–1985.* London: Collins, 1986.

Hayter, Alethea. *Charlotte Yonge.* Plymouth: Northcote House, 1996.

Heeney, Brian. *The Women's Movement in the Church of England: 1850–1930.* Oxford: Clarendon Press, 1988.

Hilton, Boyd. *The Age of Atonement: The Influence of Evangelicalism on Social and Economic Thought, 1795–1865.* Oxford: Clarendon Press, 1988.

Hinde, Wendy. *Catholic Emancipation: A Shake to Men's Minds.* Oxford: Basil Blackwell, 1992.

Houghton, E. R. "The *British Critic* and the Oxford Movement." Charlottesville: Bibliographical Society of the University of Virginia, 1963.

Hole, Robert. *Pulpits, Politics and Public Order in England, 1760–1832.* Cambridge: Cambridge University Press, 1989.

Howse, Violet. *Pusey: A Parish Record.* Oxford: Holywell Press, 1972.

Hylson-Smith, Kenneth. *High Churchmanship in the Church of England: From the Sixteenth Century to the Late Twentieth Century.* Edinburgh: T. and T. Clark, 1993.

A Hundred Years in Bengal: A History of the Oxford Mission, 1880–1980. By Two of the Brethren of the Epiphany. Delhi: ISPCK, 1979.

Imberg, Rune. *In Quest of Authority.* Lund: Lund University Press, 1987.

Inglis, K. S. *Churches and the Working Classes in Victorian England.* London: Routledge and Kegan Paul, 1963.

Jeal, Tim. *Livingstone.* Markham, Ont.: Penguin, 1985.

Jenkins, Roy. *Gladstone.* London: Macmillan, 1995.

Kenny, Terence. *The Political Thought of John Henry Newman.* London: Longmans, Green, 1957.

Ker, Ian. *John Henry Newman: A Biography.* Oxford: Oxford University Press, 1988.

Ker, Ian, and Alan G. Hill, eds. *Newman After a Hundred Years.* Oxford: Clarendon Press, 1990.

Kinzer, Bruce L., ed. *The Gladstonian Turn of Mind.* Toronto: University of Toronto Press, 1985.

Knight, Frances. *The Nineteenth-Century Church and English Society.* Cambridge: Cambridge University Press, 1995.

Liddon, H. P. *Life of Edward Bouverie Pusey.* 4 vols. London: Longmans, Green, 1893–97.

Machin, G.I.T. *The Catholic Question in English Politics, 1820 to 1830.* Oxford: Clarendon Press, 1964.

Marsh, Jan. *Christina Rossetti: A Literary Biography.* London: Jonathan Cape, 1994.

Matthew, H.C.G. *Gladstone, 1809–1874.* Oxford: Clarendon Press, 1986.

———. *Gladstone, 1875–1898.* Oxford: Clarendon Press, 1994.

McIlhiney, David B. *A Gentlemen in Every Slum: Church of England Missions in East London, 1837–1914.* Allison Park, Pa.: Pickwick Publications, 1988.

McIlvaine, Charles P. *The Chief Danger of the Church in These Times.* New York: Garland, 1843.

Mumm, Susan. *All Saints Sisters of the Poor: An Anglican Sisterhood in the Nineteenth Century.* Woodbridge: Boydell Press, 2001.

———. *Stolen Daughters, Virgin Mothers: Anglican Sisterhoods in Victorian Britain.* London: Leicester University Press, 1999.

Neill, Stephen. *A History of Christian Missions.* 2d ed. Markham, Ont.: Penguin, 1987.

Newsome, David. *The Parting of Friends: A Study of the Wilberforces and the Mannings.* Cambridge: Harvard University Press, Belknap Press, 1966.

Nockles, Peter B. *The Oxford Movement in Context: Anglican High Churchmanship, 1760–1857.* Cambridge: Cambridge University Press, 1994.

Noll, Mark A. *A History of Christianity in the United States and Canada.* Grand Rapids, Mich.: Eerdmans, 1993.

Palmer, William. *A Narrative of Events Connected with the Publication of the Tracts for the Times.* 2d ed. London: Mowbray, 1883.

Paul, Herbert. *The Life of Froude.* 2d ed. London: Pitman, 1906.

Paz, D. G. *Popular Anti-Catholicism in Mid-Victorian England.* Stanford: Stanford University Press, 1992.

Peck, William George. *The Social Implications of the Oxford Movement.* New York: Scribner's, 1934.

Phillips, Paul T. *A Kingdom on Earth: Anglo-American Social Christianity, 1880–1940.* University Park: Pennsylvania State University Press, 1996.

Pickering, W.S.F. *Anglo-Catholicism: A Study in Religious Ambiguity.* London: Mowbray, 1989.

Porter, Brian, ed. *Colonial Tractarians: The Oxford Movement in Australia.* Melbourne: Joint Board of Christian Education, 1989.

Pugin, Augustus W.N. *Contrasts: Or, a Parallel between the Noble Edifices of the Middle Ages, and Corresponding Buildings of the Present Day; Shewing the Present Decay of Taste.* London: Dolman, 1841.

Reardon, Bernard M.G. *From Coleridge to Gore: A Century of Religious Thought in Britain.* London: Longman, 1971.

Reckitt, Maurice B. *From Maurice to Temple.* London: SPCK, 1947.

Reed, John Shelton. *Glorious Battle: The Cultural Politics of Victorian Anglo-Catholicism.* Nashville: Vanderbilt University Press, 1996.

Reynolds, Michael. *Martyr of Ritualism: Father of Mackonochie of St. Alban's, Holborn.* London: Mowbray, 1965.

Rickman, Thomas. *An Attempt to Discriminate the Styles of Architecture in England, from the Conquest to the Reformation.* London: Dolman, 1817.

Rowlands, J.H.L. *Church, State and Society: The Attitudes of John Keble, Richard Hurrell Froude and John Henry Newman, 1827–1845.* Worthing, West Sussex: Churchman Publishing, 1989.

Rupp, Gordon. *Religion in England, 1688–1791.* Oxford: Clarendon Press, 1986.

Selen, Mats. *The Oxford Movement and Wesleyan Methodism in England, 1833–1882: A Study in Religious Conflict.* Lund: Lund University Press, 1992.

Shaw, G. P. *Patriarch and Patriot: William Grant Broughton, 1788–1853.* Melbourne: Melbourne University Press, 1978.

Soloway, Richard Allen. *Prelates and People: Ecclesiastical Social Thought in England, 1783–1852.* London: Routledge and Kegan Paul, 1969.

Smith, George. *Henry Martyn.* New York: F. H. Revell, 1892.

Stock, Eugene. *History of the Church Missionary Society.* 4 vols. London: Church Missionary Society, 1899–1916.

Sullivan, Alvin, ed. *British Literary Magazines: The Romantic Age, 1789–1836.* Westport, Conn.: Greenwood Press, 1983.

Thompson, H. P. *Into All Lands: The History of the Society for the Propagation of the Gospel in Foreign Parts, 1701–1900.* London: SPCK, 1951.

Toon, Peter. *Evangelical Theology, 1833–1856: A Response to Tractarianism.* London: Marshall, Morgan and Scott, 1979.

Trevor, Meriol. *Newman: The Pillar of the Cloud.* London: Macmillan, 1962.

Vaiss, Paul, ed. *From Oxford to the People: Reconsidering Newman and the Oxford Movement.* Leominster: Gracewing, 1996.

Ward, W. G. *The Ideal of a Christian Church Considered in Comparison with Existing Practice.* London: James Toovey, 1844.

Watson, J. R., ed. *An Infinite Complexity: Essays in Romanticism.* Edinburgh: University of Edinburgh Press, 1983.

Westfall, William. *Two Worlds: The Protestant Culture of Nineteenth-Century Ontario.* Montreal and Kingston: McGill-Queen's University Press, 1989.

Whately, Richard. *Introductory Lectures on Political Economy.* 2d ed. London: Fellowes, 1832.

———. *The Kingdom of Christ.* London: J. Murray, 1841.

Williams, Thomas Jay, and Allan Walter Campbell. *The Park Village Sisterhood.* London: SPCK, 1965.

Wolffe, John, ed. *Religion in Victorian Britain: Volume V, Culture and Empire.* Manchester: Manchester University Press, 1997.

Woolverton, John F. *Colonial Anglicanism in North America.* Detroit: Wayne State University Press, 1984.

Yates, Nigel. *Anglican Ritualism in Victorian Britain, 1830–1910.* Oxford: Oxford University Press, 1999.

———. "The Oxford Movement and Parish Life: St. Saviour's, Leeds, 1839–1929." University of York: Borthwick Institute, 1975.

Journal Articles

Arnold, Thomas. "The Oxford Malignants and Dr Hampden." *The Edinburgh Review* 63 (April 1836): 237–39.

Best, Geoffrey. "The Constitutional Revolution, 1828–32, and Its Consequences for the Established Church." *Theology* 62, no. 463 (1959): 226–50.

De Waal, Esther. "John Henry Hobart and the Early Oxford Movement." *Anglican Theological Review* 65, no. 3 (July 1983): 324–31.

Doll, Peter M. "American High Churchmanship and the Establishment of the First Colonial Episcopate in the Church of England: Nova Scotia, 1787." *The Journal of Ecclesiastical History* 43, no. 1 (January 1992): 35–59.

Faught, Brad. "John Charles Roper and the Oxford Movement in Toronto." *Journal of the Canadian Church Historical Society* 36, no. 2 (October 1994): 113–33.

———. "Tractarianism on the Zambesi: Bishop Mackenzie and the Beginnings of the Universities Mission to Central Africa." *Anglican and Episcopal History* 66, no. 3 (September 1997): 303–28.

Franklin, R. W. "Pusey and Worship in Industrial Society." *Worship* 57, no. 5 (September 1983): 386–412.

Kenyon, John. "The Influence of the Oxford Movement upon the Church of England in Upper Canada. " *Ontario History* 51, no. 2 (1959): 79–94.

Lynch, M. J. "Was Gladstone a Tractarian? W. E. Gladstone and the Oxford Movement, 1833–45." *Journal of Religious History* 13 (1975): 364–89.

Mandler, Peter. "Tories and Paupers: Christian Political Economy and the Making of the New Poor Law." *The Historical Journal* 33, no. 1 (1990): 81–103.

Matthew, H.C.G. "Edward Bouverie Pusey: From Scholar to Tractarian." *Journal of Theological Studies* 32 (1981): 101–24.

Ramm, Agatha. "Gladstone's Religion." *The Historical Journal* 28, no. 2 (1985): 327–40.

Reed, John Shelton. "A 'Female Movement': The Feminization of Nineteenth-Century Anglo-Catholicism." *Anglican and Episcopal History* 57, no. 2 (June 1988): 199–238.

Shook, Lawrence. "Newman's Correspondence with Two Canadians." *Dublin Review* 234 (Autumn 1960): 205–21.

Unpublished Dissertations

Faught, Curtis Brad. "The Oxford Movement and Politics: Church and State and Social Action." Ph.D. diss., University of Toronto, 1996.

Herring, George William. "Tractarianism to Ritualism: A Study of Some Aspects of Tractarianism Outside Oxford, From the Time of Newman's Conversion in 1845, Until the First Ritual Commission in 1867." D. Phil. thesis, University of Oxford, 1984.

Nockles, Peter B. "Continuity and Change in British High Churchmanship, 1792–1850." D. Phil. thesis, University of Oxford, 1982.

Tinsley, Beverly A.B. "John Henry Newman and the *British Critic*." Ph.D. diss., Northwestern University, 1972.

Novels

Disraeli, Benjamin. *Coningsby, Or the New Generation*. Ed. Thom Braun. Markham, Ont.: Penguin, 1983.

———. *Sybil, Or the Two Nations*. Ed. Sheila M. Smith. New York: Oxford University Press, 1991.

Index